MODERN CORPORATE MANAGEMENT:

New Approaches to
Financial Control,
Operations, Customer
Development,
and Equity Sources

WALTER N. KUNTZ

PRENTICE-HALL, INC.   Englewood Cliffs, N.J.

*To the memory of my wife,
Kay, in gratitude for the
bright light of her days.*

Prentice-Hall International, Inc., *London*
Prentice-Hall of Australia, Pty. Ltd., *Sydney*
Prentice-Hall of Canada, Ltd., *Toronto*
Prentice-Hall of India Private Ltd., *New Delhi*
Prentice-Hall of Japan, Inc., *Tokyo*
Whitehall Books, Ltd., *Wellington, New Zealand*
Prentice-Hall of Southeast Asia Pte. Ltd., *Singapore*

© 1978 by

Prentice-Hall, Inc.
Englewood Cliffs, N.J.

Library of Congress Cataloging in Publication Data

Kuntz, Walter N.
   Modern corporate management.

   Includes index.
   1. Industrial management. 2. Corporations--
Finance. I. Title.
HD31.K83   658.4   78-1386
ISBN 0-13-589754-8

Printed in the United States of America

ABOUT THE AUTHOR

Walter N. Kuntz is a lifelong professional manager with both line and staff experience in operations, financial management, sales, inventory control and general management. He has been President of the Southwestern Drug Corporation, Senior Vice-President of the Brunswig Drug Company, and Senior Vice-President of the Bergen Brunswig Corporation, being an Executive Committee member and Director of Southwestern and Bergen Brunswig while serving as an officer of those organizations. Mr. Kuntz continues his association as Director of Bergen Brunswig where he chairs the Executive Compensation and Stock Option Committee, as well. He is also consultant to the Southwestern Drug Corporation, Sav-On Drugs and the Bergen Brunswig Corp. in Texas.

A frequent speaker before national business meetings and conventions, Mr. Kuntz has been a lecturer at a number of seminars, appearing as feature speaker before professional and educational groups.

The author has been awarded an LLB degree from the Houston Law School and is a graduate of the FBI Academy. He is licensed as an attorney and counselor-at-law in Texas and admitted and qualified as an Attorney & Counsellor of the Supreme Court of the United States.

FOREWORD

Since the discovery of the wheel, man has been tinkering with it to learn why it works, where, when, how and for whom it functions. This curiosity has encouraged the rampant technology of the early part of the twentieth century, culminating in the quest for distribution of products in the middle of the century. The last score of years in this century must be dedicated to tidying up the grounds and rules of producing and supplying the wants and needs of the universe. This is called *management*.

Management has been the least cultivated of business talents. Competition has had its way in creating products and moving them to market. Competition is now in the forefront for honing management capability to a fine edge.

The stakes in enterprise currently are too massive for amateur approaches—the prospects for failure through management myopia are too great to fail to comprehend the absolute necessity of educated, professional judgments about use of money, the efficient operation, the measure and development of customers and the control of growth.

The answers, the techniques and the procedures suggested in *Modern Corporate Management* are not ivy-covered theories, but, rather, the tested realities that have been fired and hardened in the furnace of experience by the author—who with charming subtlety says that he is not a professional writer, but a professional manager.

A journey through these pages, to be often re-visited, is a post-graduate experience in what the business world needs most—skilled management techniques.

—Walter Cousins, Jr.

A WORD FROM THE AUTHOR

This book was written to assist management in bringing fresh approaches to old problems and for use as new questions arise.

Divided, as it is, into four parts,

I FINANCIAL CONTROL

II OPERATIONS

III CUSTOMER DEVELOPMENT

IV EQUITY SOURCES

this book is actually four books in one.

The thrust of the book is the presentation of proven management techniques that get results, *new and modern approaches*. It concentrates on those special techniques that generate desired results without increasing equity investment requirements. There are no simple answers in management; there are only intelligent solutions. This book is a working tool that provides those solutions.

One company with an above industry-average performance in all operating areas and already at a high plateau of efficiency, initiated every new management technique outlined in this book over a five year period with the following results during that period.

NET SHIPMENTS (SALES) well above the SUBJECT COMPANY's previous record and far above the industry averages and that of the market serviced.	increased	+ 85%
EARNINGS BEFORE TAXES	increased	+ 180%
R.O.I.	increased	+ 189%
OPERATING EXPENSES	declined	− 30%

NUMBER OF EMPLOYEES	declined	− 13%
INVENTORY TURNS	increased	+ 22%
DAYS RECEIVABLES	declined	− 33%
AVERAGE ACCOUNT SIZE	increased	+209%
TOTAL SQUARE FOOTAGE	was reduced	− 13%
SALES PER SQUARE FOOT	increased	+114%

These accomplishments were not made as academic field tests. There is no academia here. This is the record of a large, publicly owned company operating in a highly competitive field with alert, aggressive management, always looking for a better way while operating under the competitive pressures that test the realities of every new management procedure. The new management procedures outlined in this book stood up under the grind of practical competitive daily use and the overall results far exceeded expectations.

Isn't this what you want?

1. *More sales*
2. *Higher earnings*
3. *Increased R.O.I.*
4. *Reduced operating expenses*
5. *Fewer, more efficient employees*
6. *Less inventory investment and a higher rate of turn*
7. *Fewer days outstanding on your receivables*
8. *Larger, more profitable accounts to service*
9. *Compressed or reduced office and warehouse space for less costly and more efficient operation*
10. *More sales per square foot.*

Every company objective was met in this 10 point profit improvement program.

This is an excellent example of how this book can help you. It presents new approaches to old problems and they get you the results you want.

Each chapter contains a number of actual working examples of the new management procedure discussed in that chapter. The comparison periods vary from quarterly comparisons, six months, annual or more, depending on the period of time the Subject Company or companies have been using the procedure. All examples are of operating companies with experienced management. All are familiar with the realities of competitive pressures in today's market place. Examples, selected at random, reflect a high level of uniform improvement which is usually evident in the very early months of operation after initiating the new management concept or procedure. The improvement generally is as dramatic as the five year example already outlined for you in some detail. While the benefits have a cumulative effect, you don't have to wait five years to get them. Improvement is evident in the first few months or first quarter of usage.

Every modern corporate management technique presented for your consideration and use has as its ultimate objective, the more efficient use of equity capital. Management with the capacity to improve return on investment will be the dominant and most sought after management during the next decade. This book helps you provide that kind of management.

Keep the book on your desk and use it daily. Do not have an index card made and assign it to space on a shelf in the company library. Time is of the essence. *The book should be put to work now!*

No material has been presented in this book that cannot withstand the most relentless scrutiny as well as stand up under the constant pressure of daily use.

No part of this book has been taken from the writings of others. There is no bibliography for that reason.

The acknowledgements section is extensive and complete in listing the contributors to this book. Review it carefully. The thinking, creativity and skills of this illustrious group of experienced management and administrative people will serve you well in planning and executing new management techniques in the '80s, and for decades to follow. Looking ahead at the next ten years, and at the new and varied demands that will be made upon management, quite a different picture emerges than the one we saw in the '60s. Then, merger and acquisition experts dominated the business scene. And such terms as "diversification" and "conglomerate" were in common usage. The "wheeler-dealers," with the talent and the persuasiveness to merge and acquire businesses, did not always demonstrate the management capability to operate them profitably nor to plan long range, efficient use of equity. Price/earnings ratios of highly diversified companies or conglomerates began to drop sharply and investors realized that nothing is gained when a merger or acquisition results in making a company only bigger and not better. It was inevitable that the '70s would see successful management switch to the field of *Operations*. It did.

Just as the '70s required skilled operations management, *The '80s will belong to management with the capacity to make the most efficient use of equity. That is what this book is all about*—to give reliable direction to your efforts to attain the most important business goals of the next decade. You will find 15 ways that this book will help you manage more effectively.

In PART I of the book, FINANCE, a simple management technique is outlined that more than doubles return on investment. You pull your investment requirements down to the lowest possible levels. This is Chapter 1. A new technique that reduces operating costs and boosts sales volume is outlined in Chapter 2. Chapter 3 describes proven ways to boost productivity without increasing capital requirements or raising prices. And Chapter 4 provides a practical review of new techniques in data entry and information retrieval systems, all information you need to have now.

Moving to PART II, OPERATIONS, we have three chapters that outline specific, workable procedures for cutting operating costs in half and keeping them there, decreasing inventory by identifying and eliminating "non-moving" items from stock, and increasing sales up to 50% and more. All are actual case history results.

In PART III of the book, CUSTOMER DEVELOPMENT, we review three new ways to build more productive, viable, profitable, prompt paying customers. All are documented by actual case history results.

In PART IV, EQUITY SOURCES, we take "the long look" at such areas as,

- Coping with problems of reorganization
- Going public and other forms of permanent financing

- Financial planning as part of corporate planning
- Operational use of short range management by objective.

The author takes a close, analytical look at the attributes and characteristics of THE PERCEPTIVE DIRECTOR. Schedules for THE IMPLEMENTATION OF NEW MANAGEMENT TECHNIQUES outlined in the book are considered. And, since opportunities still exist in the area of mergers and acquisitions, there are unique situations that can be found and should be evaluated that could nourish the "green edge of growth" of your company in the years ahead.

As an experienced C.E.O., you will appreciate the practical approach of this book. The format:

This is what we do when . . .
Here is how we do it . . .
These are the results . . .

HOW THIS BOOK CAN HELP YOU may be evaluated if you would like to improve your company's performance in any of the 10 operating categories reported in the preceding example.

We did not list the dollars and cents in this particular part of the preliminary text but earnings increased in this example at the rate of *a million dollars a year*, the fifth year reflecting a five million dollar increase over the first year.

Total sales moved from just under *two hundred million* a year the first year to approximately *three hundred fifty million in the fifth year*. So, we are talking about *millions of dollars* in this example.

Earnings before taxes moved from just under *three million* in the first year to approximately *eight million* in the fifth year, *a gain averaging a million a year* as we have stated.

We are giving you in this book a set of new management procedures that can mean millions of dollars of increased earnings to your firm. See CHAPTER 18, RESULTS for a complete factual performance record of Subject Company "E".

Other chapters will tell you how these accomplishments were made without increasing equity investment but on the contrary, reducing equity requirements.

Doesn't this formula appeal to you and wouldn't it also be attractive to your shareholders? Your answer has to be "Yes." Remember again that these are not untried procedures that are proposed but actual new modern corporate management techniques already proven and now at work reducing equity requirements and increasing corporate earnings. To reduce corporate equity requirements and to increase corporate sales and earnings, put this book to work. The proven procedures outlined will generate substantial dividends in your operations.

It is the purpose of this book to unlock doors of knowledge that will prove to be useful in your business, and to invite you to confidently make use of the new management techniques behind those doors that have aroused your curiosity. This is the invitation. And this, in a sense, will be your reward for buying and *using* this book.

Walter N. Kuntz

ACKNOWLEDGMENTS

In compiling and preparing the chapters of this book, I have felt a growing awareness of how much each one of us in management is educated, developed and inspired by our peer associates in business.

This environment makes a heavy contribution to our professional management growth.

A broad and exceptionally creative environment fortunately can be extended to educate, develop and inspire others not immediately associated with those men responsible for the ideas, the inspiration and the perseverance that result in effective creative management.

This book is a means of extending and sharing that environment.

This book could never have been created by one person alone. In addition to what I myself was able to contribute from my own experience in management as well as in handling directorate responsibilities, I have used a great deal of material that is, in reality, the product of other men, exceptionally qualified, creative people with whom I have been and/or am now associated.

It has been my privilege to be in the company of Olympians during much of my business life. These men are all contributors to this book. Each man at one time or another during the half century 1925-1975, demonstrated the creative ability, management capacity or the required administrative skills to develop and apply those timely innovations that enable business enterprises to prosper and endure. It is a diverse but select group of men.

The users of this book are invited to share their thinking and creative ability with the author who gratefully acknowledges the special privileges involved. And so together we expand and broaden our business environment to include them:

SINCLAIR ARMSTRONG, Executive Vice President, U.S. Trust Company or New York, and former Chairman, Securities and Exchange Commission.

DR. RODNEY H. BRADY, an Executive Vice President of the Bergen Brunswig Corp., Director and Executive Committee Member and a former Vice President of the Hughes Tool Company.

STANTON BROWN, SR.,° Former Chairman of the Board, Exporters & Traders Compress & Warehouse Company; a founder of the Southwestern Drug Corporation; Director and Executive Committee Member.

WALTER H. COUSINS, JR., Former Editor and Publisher of the Southern Pharmaceutical Journal - Dallas; former City Commission and Mayor pro tem, Dallas; Later Editor of Drug Topics and Drug Trade News, New York; Lecturer in residence, Texas University, Austin, Texas.

LEO J. DiSTEFANO, Executive Vice-President Drug Distribution-West, Bergen Brunswig Corporation.

FRED FLORENCE*, Former Board Chairman, Republic National Bank of Dallas, Texas.

JOHN EDGAR HOOVER*, Former Director of the Federal Bureau of Investigation, United States Department of Justice, Washington, D.C.

CLIFTON C. HOPPER, President and Board Chairman, Southwestern Drug Corporation.

W. C. ("DECKER") JACKSON, JR., Investment Banker, Chairman of the Board, First Southwest Company, Dallas, Texas; Past President, Investment Bankers Association of America; Chairman of the Board, Municipal Advisory Council of Texas; President and Director of Antelope Oil Corporation; Director, Provident Oil Co.

GAINER B. JONES, Senior Vice-President, and Loan Officer (retired) - National Bank of Commerce, Houston (now Texas Commerce Bank).

JESSE H. JONES°, Board Chairman, National Bank of Commerce Houston; Director of Reconstruction Finance Corporation under Hoover; Chairman of the Reconstruction Finance Corporation under Roosevelt. Former Secretary of Commerce and author of the book *Fifty Billion Dollars*, a story of the RFC.

JAMES W. KEAY, Chairman of the Board, Republic National Bank of Dallas, Texas.

RUSSEL G. KOENEMAN, Professional Designer-Consultant, Houston and San Antonio, Texas.

WALTER N. KUNTZ, III, Partner in the law firm of Akin, Gump, Strauss, Hauer & Feld, with offices in Dallas, Texas and Washington, D.C.

EMIL P. MARTINI, JR., President, Chairman of the Board and Chief Executive Officer of the Bergen Brunswig Corporation.

ROBERT E. MARTINI, an Executive Vice-President and Director of the Bergen Brunswig Corporation.

W.A. ("AL") PARISH*, Partner, Baker & Botts, Houston; Director of Southwestern Drug Corporation and Houston Lighting & Power Co.

C.M. "BOOTS" PENLAND*, a founder and first executive Vice-President of the Southwestern Drug Corporation; Director and Executive Committee Member.

G.H. "HARVE" PENLAND*, First Chairman of the Board of Directors of the Southwestern Drug Corporation; Director and Executive Committee Member and a founder; former Attorney General, M.K.T. Railway Co.

ACKNOWLEDGMENTS

J.M. "JIM" PENLAND*, a founder and the first President and Chief Executive Officer of the Southwestern Drug Corporation.

WALTER P. ROZETT, Executive Vice President, Envirotech Corp., Menlo Park, California.

ROY V. SCHWAB*, Former Board Chairman of the Brunswig Drug Company, California.

E.V. STAUDE, Former President of the Brunswig Drug Company, California.

BEN H. STEVENS°, a founder of the Magnolia Oil Company, now part of Mobil Oil Company, organized and managed the Petroleum Board under United States Department of Interior Secretary Harold Ickes. Director, Executive Committee Member, Southwestern Drug Corporation.

ANTHONY VALLARIO, Group Vice-President—Computer Services, Bergen Brunswig Corporation, and a leading national authority on computer system applications in business today.

I would also like to thank the National Wholesale Druggists Association of Scarsdale, N.Y. for their kind permission to use the official N.W.D.A. presidential portrait by W.H. Anderson.

*Deceased

Contents

17

PART TWO: OPERATIONS
Three New Procedures That Cut Operating Costs In Half and Keep Them There

PART III: CUSTOMER DEVELOPMENT
Three New Ways to Build More Productive, Viable, Profitable, Prompt Paying Customers

PART IV: EQUITY SOURCES
Corporate Planning and Financial Planning: Appraisal, Development and the Use of People

PART ONE
FINANCIAL CONTROL

Four Proven Ways to Improve Internal Financial Control and Equity Investment Requirements

1

THE COST OF MONEY CHARGE: A TECHNIQUE THAT MORE THAN DOUBLES RETURN ON INVESTMENT

An innovative technique that multiplies return on investment—is simple to apply and meets with enthusiastic acceptance by division management as a substitute for the old arbitrary corporate allocation charge.

THE CHALLENGE

The "cost of money charge" is a totally new management technique that eliminates all negatives inherent in old corporate expense allocation methods based on a percent of sales formula.

When the allocation method is replaced by a controllable expense item, the "cost of money charge," at the branch or division level, the results are:

- beneficial, and
- immediate.

The "cost of money charge" provides Division Management with incentives to:

- reduce inventories,
- reduce accounts receivable,
- improve return on division investment.

Any business operating a number of divisions is confronted with the need to distribute general office costs or corporate allocations to its operating divisions. Traditionally this has been handled through the use of a percent of total sales formula. The disadvantages of this procedure are too well known to enumerate here. Separate and somewhat different formulae for distribution and manufacturing are set out in this chapter.

The problem centers around the arbitrary nature of the charge. The charge provides operating division management with arithmetic that it is curious about, but cannot and does not use constructively. It is an uncontrollable item of expense at the division level. It is often substantial in relation to other division operating expense items. The charge is usually resented; it is objected to vocally by some division managers and borne in silence but with equal resentment by others. Businesses have continued to use the old percentage of sale allocation method simply because management has not seriously considered anything better.

HERE IS SOMETHING BETTER!

Cease allocating general office or corporate expenses in relation to sales volume. Make a "cost of money charge" to all operating divisions each month.

Get away from the negatives of saddling operating divisions with arbitrary corporate monthly expense charges or allocations over which division management has no control. Substitute an incentive program that rewards more efficient use of capital employed in the business.

What specifically is the "cost of money charge"?

How is it calculated?

Where are the incentives?

How does it really work?

What are the results?

The "cost of money charge" is a monthly charge of 1% of "net assets" used by the division. The percentage per month can be any justifiable percentage that fits your operations. There is nothing arbitrary about the 1% per month figure although it is simple to compute and fits most distribution operations.

1% per month is much easier for the Division Manager, Buyer, Warehouse Superintendent or Credit Manager to understand. Each one of these men can make his own computation. All he has to do is move the decimal place. Even the most unsosphisticated businessman can readily understand this procedure and quickly comprehend the consequences in added operating costs through the "cost of money charge" increases that occur when inventories and/or accounts receivable increase.

"Net assets" for the purpose of this charge, in the distribution field, are defined as:

1. inventory investment less accounts payable
2. accounts receivable

Why define inventory investment as inventory *less payables*? This arrangement encourages division management and/or buyers to ask for maximum available legal terms including "*dating*" offered at intervals by suppliers on promotional items or lines. A supplier's or vendor's money, if purchases are discounted within agreed terms, is a desirable source of cost free capital. Use it. Buying on 30-day terms and taking advantage of "dating" purchases when available, while selling on 15-day terms, provides opportunities for suppliers to use vendors' money (payables) as a legitimate source of operating capital. This technique reduces the need for equity capital or bank borrowing. This procedure makes a significant contribution to increasing return on investment ratios, in some instances pushing them up to the highest possible levels. See examples to follow.

Division inventory figures from month to month are, of course, estimates. There is no need for monthly physical inventory since division gross profit figures generally follow a consistent pattern.

Accounts payable outstanding figures are taken from the division trial balance or balance sheet. If a central payable system is used, it is a simple matter to monitor payables by divisions and extract each division figure.

The accounts receivable totals each month are simply trial balance figures.

The charge of 1% of net assets used by each division is made:

- to eliminate any difference among operations because some locations are owned and others are leased.
- to simplify the allocation and relate it directly to current performance of the division.
- to emphasize and encourage sound management of the assets of the company.

Specifically, the charge directly reflects inventory management and accounts receivable collection efforts. The 1% charge is in lieu of all other corporate costs.

In effect, it is saying that the cost of maintaining the parent company is essentially related to the cost of raising money.

The 1% per month charge or 12% per year does not represent what it costs to borrow or otherwise provide money for the operating division.

Your company can and probably does borrow money at the prime rate (a variable factor) but it can only borrow about half of what is necessary to finance the business. The other half is provided by shareholders' investment plus "after tax" and "after dividend liability" retained earnings.

If we average the half that comes from borrowing with the half that comes from shareholders, it is obvious that the cost of money exceeds the 1% per month "cost of money charge" or 12% per year. And this is before considering other corporate expenses.

Another basic objective behind the 1% "cost of money charge," is, among other things, to help establish a perspective on the company, on the operating locations, and most importantly, on management itself. It provides an opportunity for division managers to demonstrate sensitivity to return on investment—consisting of profits and their relationship to the amount of money subject to their control—required to generate those profits.

The 1% factor in effect becomes a corporate statement of the kind of effort looked for in controlling the amount of investment. It is not to be accepted by Division Managers as a mechanical routine allocation but rather as a communications device that will help a manager understand what is expected of him as a minimum.

A company, to attract investors, must be in a position to offer earnings of 10% on an investment (after corporate taxes).

Efficient use of capital is the essential that the new "cost of money charge" is all about, and instilling this concept at the division management levels is of critical importance.

Using some of your own branch or division arithmetic, calculate the effect of the "cost of money charge" compared with the "percent of sales allocation" method. Project relative percentages of these charges in relation to sales and watch with satisfaction the declining demand for equity capital on the part of your operating divisions to sustain present sales volume levels as well as to handle normal sales increases projected in line with company plans or objectives.

Return on capital used in the business improves impressively as more efficient use of money invested in division inventories and receivables makes it possible for divisions to handle sales increases without requiring disproportionate investments of equity capital.

The Division Manager "grapevine" topic can now change from the negative approach of trying to calculate the total corporate expense allocations to see how much this or that item may be increasing while "pressure continues on us, the operating divisions, to decrease or hold the line on operating costs", to "how do you get your 'cost of money charge' down so low and sustain your sales'?"

The "cost of money charge" procedure results in a completely changed outlook in the area of corporate allocation, a better one for all concerned, including shareholders. It is a simple, basic procedure, easily implemented with far-reaching, beneficial results.

RESULTS

Return on Investment After "Cost of Money Charges" and Before Taxes

Example "A" — Last Quarter Comparative Results— Ten Operating Divisions

	Last Fiscal Year (last quarter)	Current Fiscal Year (last quarter)
Division #1	35.4	67.3
Division #2	33.1	60.4
Division #3	41.4	48.1
Division #4	37.3	47.8
Division #5	30.1	39.0
Division #6	24.5	37.2
Division #7	24.0	32.6
Division #8	9.4	30.4
Division #9	17.3	30.0
Division #10	9.5	24.5

"Return on equity" or "return on investment" is always stated "before taxes." There is no "after tax" column in the above example, nor will there be in other examples to follow, for three reasons:

1. The disparity in "after tax" figures due to varying organizational structures. All companies reported are not structured alike. Some may be corporations, others partnerships, and still others, proprietorships.
2. In other instances, tax credits carried forward create distorted "after tax" figures.
3. All multi-division operations do not break down the net "after tax" earnings by divisions, but use a consolidated figure.

Uniform comparisons can be obtained simply by dividing the return on investment percentages by two, since taxes, on average, are equal to approximately 50% of operating profit figures. While "net assets" are defined as inventory investment less accounts payable plus accounts receivable, for purposes of calculating "cost of money charges," the return on investment figures set out under the caption "results" are the actual return on investment after "cost of money charges" and "before taxes." In these calculations, return on each total division investment is reflected. The special definition of "net assets" applies only to the basis for "cost of money charge" calculations. The ROI figures listed are actual before tax percentages based on total equity invested in each division.

Return on equity is something else and we will discuss the relationship in some detail. The purpose of this example arithmetic is to provide a simple and direct road to improved return on equity by reducing controllable equity requirements of the business and improved earnings in relation to those requirements.

If it is a publicly owned company, this is a procedure that can also result in an improved price for listed company stocks.

There is an old "bench mark" that in effect says "you can convert your return on equity into your price-earnings ratio." If you can deliver 8%, after tax, your stock will sell for 64% of book value (8% x 8). You must make a minimum of 10% in order to sell at your book value; that is essential for survival. If you deliver 15% return on equity, you can expect your stock to sell for about 1½ times your book value, and that is what success and growth are really built on.

Any company's stock itself is a commodity, the price of which is determined by what a buyer is willing to pay and at which an owner is willing to sell. Many other factors affect the price of stock, as we all know, but this formula has merit.

All divisions reflect earnings in relation to investment as being substantially greater after implementing the "cost of money charge" program. Earnings from Divisions #1 and #2 are almost double; Divisions #8 and #10 reflect dramatic improvements.

The Managers of Divisions #8 and #10 had two problems last year:

1. Each Manager insisted upon carrying many infrequently ordered items in stock to accommodate certain "key accounts," large volume customers who would from time to time buy those items. When each Manager realized what it cost his operation to provide these "accommodation items," he realized that his "key customers" handling those same items, all of which had been replaced in the market by newer and improved products, must be experiencing the same costs. The Managers, working with each salesman involved,

called on those customers and explained that it was a costly procedure for them to continue to stock obsolete items for the convenience of a few consumers who occasionally bought them. They suggested that efforts should be made to interest those consumers in the newer and improved products that had replaced the old ones in the market. This was, in the main, successfully done. The slow moving or exceptional items were, for the most part, eliminated from Divisions #8 and #10's inventories. There was no sales attrition experienced by either division or by the retailers involved because a sound constructive selling job had been done. The retailers had succeeded in selling the consumers a new and improved version of an old item for which general demand had ceased.

2. The other problem was an accounts receivable one. There were a number of "loyal," long-time customers, high volume accounts in each division; the divisions had for years been carrying 60 to 90 day purchases on the books for those accounts. Here again, each manager took a look at his costs of carrying those accounts, the cost of money charge, and another selling job was done. The salesman assigned to each account, working with the Financial Services Manager, set up a program to gradually bring each account into a current position over a period of months. See Chapter on "Planned Profit Programs for Customers" and "The Financial Services Manager—a New Concept for the Old Credit Manager."

Lack of supervision over one or the other of the following management controls, followed by remedial action, released funds that were used to gradually work each customer account back into current status.

1. Inventory Control

Several customers had been buying more than "cost of sales" for months and even years and carried excessive and increasing inventories.

2. Accounts Receivable Control

Some problem customers lacked proper supervision over their own accounts receivable. Methods of opening new accounts were reviewed. Prompt statement mailing schedules were set up where needed; monthly aged analysis of accounts were prepared for use in following up those accounts reflecting delinquent balances, with tactful, fair and effective collection efforts.

3. Operating Expenses

Some customers failed to exercise the proper supervision over controllable items of expense; excessive proprietor's withdrawals were a predominate problem and a touchy one. Delivery costs and advertising expenses were out of hand in many stores. Corrective action by store management made funds available for a gradual monthly reduction program through which delinquent debt was worked out.

Many stores had a combination of these problems and others. None were beyond remedial handling.

In the last quarter of the current fiscal year, Divisions #8 and #10 have a much better current accounts receivable position than at the same period last year.

These are some of the reasons why return on investment after cost of money charges and before taxes moved from a low 9.4% to 30.4% in Division #8 compared to the same period of the previous year, and from 9.5% to 24.5% in Division #10. Similar but less dramatic improvement occurred in other Divisions.

Division Management's sensitivity to return on investment improves a great deal when Managers understand their responsibility as not simply improving Division profits as a percent of sales, but improving earnings on the money or investment required to sustain their division's operation. Divisions #8 and #10 should double their first quarter figure by fiscal year's end. This would bring them in line with the better divisions' performances.

A shareholder is not concerned about profits as a percent of sale. He is interested only in profits as a percent of investment, specifically, his investment. In reviewing quarterly and annual reports, shareholders tend to scan operating statements and go directly to the earnings per share numbers.

Since the Division Manager, like "top management," actually works for the shareholders, what's wrong with the Division Manager having that same perspective? Why shouldn't he share the responsibility for efficient use of equity capital with "top management"? He should and does under the "cost of money charge" and learns to control it. Division Managers expand their interest beyond sales and operations and cease relying upon the corporate office as an endless source of money or equity capital which they feel no direct responsibility for providing. When they do, Division Managers tend to hold their money requirements down. The "cost of money charge" creates sensitivity to the cost of money employed in the business and brings Division Management into a more responsible position for the use of capital invested in each division, specifically, his division.

Without pursuing example arithmetic in endless detail by division, in Example "A":

Sales increased an average of 9.5 to 10% in each division.

Inventory turnover improved from 7.4 turns to 8.1 turns. The industry average is 6.25 turns.

Accounts receivable days outstanding dropped from 38 days to 33 days, down 5 days and much better than the industry average.

Percentage of inventory financed by suppliers increased 6%, moving from 70% in the prior fiscal year to 76% in the current fiscal year.

This was a vast increase in "cost free" working capital; it had a very favorable effect on increased return on investment percentages after "cost of money charges" as set out in the preceding schedule listed in Example "A" operating ten divisions.

Material improvement in earnings relative to investment is again reflected in the example operation. Again, these percentages are based on operating profits before taxes as a percentage of division investments.

More examples reflecting full year comparisons of division receivables and inventory investments after "cost of money charge" implementations are now available and are set out in considerable detail for your study and comparison.

Return on Investment After
"Cost of Money" Charges and Before Taxes

Example "B" — Five Operating Divisions

	Last Fiscal Year (last quarter)	Current Fiscal Year (last quarter)
Division #1	39.7	64.3
Division #2	22.2	53.4
Division #3	26.0	44.1
Division #4	26.0	42.9
Division #5	23.8	30.9

LOOK AT THESE RESULTS

Accounts Receivable Days Outstanding on 15 Day Terms

[Semi-monthly statements mailed on last day of month; payable 10th and on the 15th; payable the 25th]

Subject Company "A"

DIVISION	DAYS OUTSTANDING Prior Year	Current Year	Charges + or −
A	26	23	3 −
B	28	24	4 −
C	22	23	1 +
D	28	23	5 −
E	31	26	5 −
F	29	25	4 −
G	22	26	4 +
H	29	26	3 −
I	26	26	-0-
J	29	28	1 −

Total Reduction of Days Sales Outstanding on Receivables   20 −

This new pattern reduced equity requirements of Subject Company "A" by approximately one million dollars ($1,000,000.00) with division sales increases averaging between 10% and 12% per division.

Reductions were accomplished by collecting "non-current" or "delinquent" balances primarily.

Accounts Receivable Days Outstanding on 30 Day Terms*

[Statements mailed at month's end, payable the 10th of the following month]

Subject Company "B"

DIVISION	DAYS OUTSTANDING Prior Year	Current Year	Charges + or −
A*	32	24	8 −
B	33	35	2 +
C	33	32	1 −
D*	30	22	8 −
E*	60	47	13 −
F*	51	25	26 −
G*	57	13	44 −
H	21	19	2 −

Total Reduction of Days Sales Outstanding on Receivables   100*

*It should be noted that in Divisions A, D, E, F and G, some major accounts were converted to a "pay by invoice basis." This change, plus elimination of "dating" sales and the bringing into a current position of a number of accounts with substantial delinquent balances, resulted in an abnormal reduction in days sales outstanding during the current year.

Equity requirements to carry receivables were dramatically reduced.

Good sales increases were experienced by the divisions, well over the industry average and in the 10% range.

Accounts Receivable Days Outstanding on 30 Day Terms

[Statements mailed at month's end, payable the 10th approximately]

Subject Company "C"

DIVISION	DAYS OUTSTANDING Prior Year	Current Year	Charges + or −
A	41	30	11 −
B	41	30	11 −
C	41	30	11 −

Total Reduction of Days Sales Outstanding on Receivables   33

CASE IN POINT

Customers who pay promptly tend to buy more!

Every Division of the several subject companies showing substantial reductions in receivables (much of which had been delinquent) experienced sales increases of from 10% to 12%, well above the industry average.

Subject Company "C" reduced equity requirements for receivables by approximately a half million dollars.

**Accounts Receivable Days Outstanding
on 30 Day Terms**

[Statements mailed at month's end,
payable the 10th of the following month]

Subject Company "D"

DIVISION	DAYS OUTSTANDING *Prior Year*	*Current Year*	*Charges* *+ or −*
A	38	27	11 −
B	37	30	7 −
C	27	25	2 −
D	39	31	8 −
Total Reduction of Days Sales Outstanding on Receivables			28 −

Here's what happened to equity requirements in one year:

Translated into dollars we have an equity requirement reduction of approximately $400,000.00.

Check this:

Another major equity requirement is inventory investment. How did the subject companies fare in handling this control?

With a sales increase experience ranging from 10% to 12%, rate of inventory turnover increased and days on hand generally went down.

See following schedules.

HERE ARE THE FIGURES FOR SUBJECT COMPANY "A":

Division	Prior Year Days on Hand	T/O	Current Year Days on Hand	T/O
A	37.4	9.8	37.4	9.8
B	35.8	10.2	33.1	11.0
C	45.6	8.0	41.8	8.7
D	53.3	6.8	46.4	7.9
E	41.0	8.9	41.5	8.8
F	55.6	6.6	39.3	9.3
G	45.8	8.0	42.8	8.5
H	49.3	7.4	34.4	10.6
I	46.1	7.9	37.8	9.7
J	37.8	9.7	46.1	7.9
All Divisions	44.76	8.33	39.9	9.22

HERE IS THE COMPARABLE INVENTORY INVESTMENT AND TURNOVER POSITION OF SUBJECT COMPANY "B":

Division	Prior Year Days on Hand	T/O	Current Year Days on Hand	T/O
A	60.8	6.0	60.3	6.1
B	71.7	5.1	62.7	5.8
C	44.9	8.1	46.6	7.8
D	47.4	7.7	47.5	7.7
E	33.1	11.0	35.8	10.2
F	41.8	8.7	46.4	7.9
G	41.5	8.8	41.0	8.9
H	39.3	9.3	47.7	7.7
All Divisions	47.39	8.1	48.17	7.8

SUBJECT COMPANY "C" HAS THESE COMPARABLE INVENTORY INVESTMENT AND TURNOVER RECORDS:

Year Division	Prior Year Days on Hand	T/O	Current Year Days on Hand	T/O
A	44.1	8.3	46.8	7.8
B	46.0	7.9	44.3	8.2
C	68.6	5.8	51.5	7.1
All Divisions	52.9	7.3	47.5	7.7

THE "DAYS ON HAND" AND TURNOVER FIGURES FOR SUBJECT COMPANY "D":

[30 day terms—statements mailed at
month end, payable the 10th of the following month]

Division	Prior Year Days on Hand	T/O	Current Year Days on Hand	T/O
A	44.1	8.3	46.8	7.8
B	46.0	7.9	44.3	8.2
C	68.0	5.8	51.5	7.1
All Divisions	52.7	7.3	47.5	7.7

Here are many working examples, taken from audited schedules and work papers, that clearly reflect reduced equity requirements (reduced accounts receivable and inventory investments). These result when Division Management, sales, buyers and inventory control people understand the basic principle involved in the "cost of money charge". An awareness of the cost of carrying excessive receivables and inventories will get the results you must have to efficiently use company equity investment in the '80s, when your equity investment must be effectively controlled to handle the increased sales volume you plan to develop. Control of equity is not an impediment to sales. Delinquent accounts and money invested in slow moving items do not improve sales.

Here are many examples that clearly show that equity investments in accounts receivable and inventories do decline, even in the face of rising sales, if Division Management effectively communicates the fact that:

1. every dollar in receivables carried beyond maturity, and

2. every dollar invested in slow moving items in inventory costs the division money and becomes a deterrent to division profitability. On the other hand, control of inventories and receivables boosts earnings materially.

The preceding examples of favorable results attained through the use of the new cost of money charge based on net assets (defined as inventory investment, less payables plus accounts receivable for purposes of this calculation), instead of a pro rata distribution of corporate costs formula based on sales, are primarily business engaged in distribution.

Applied to multi-unit retail operations, comparable results are experienced; equity requirements decline.

Examples of improved results at retail are much too numerous to describe here in detail, but there is an impressive parallel with the numerous examples reported in the distribution operations. The same definition of "net assets" (inventory less accounts payable plus accounts receivable) for purposes of calculating the "cost of money charge" used in distribution is also applied at retail. The percentage charged each month is a variable, depending upon the corporate general office structure, services provided and number of units in operation. More supervision and services performed for fewer units require a higher rate of "cost of money charge" but the principle is the same and it works. There is nothing "sacred" about the 1% per month figure; however, it fits most operations, is simple to calculate, and is easily and quickly understood.

In the manufacturing field, corporate cost allocations frequently run much higher than 1% of sales. In some instances, where a manufacturer is engaged in producing large pieces of equipment or infrequently sold large units, the figure may be 5% of sales or higher. In some instances it may be as high as 10% or 12%. Sales of the item manufactured may be sporadic or seasonal. The same general "cost of money charge" formula may be used with one or two modifications. Add "equipment investment" to "inventory less payables plus accounts receivable" and divide inventory into two (2) categories:

(a) raw materials or unfinished products, containers, labels, etc.; and
(b) finished inventory.

A third inventory (c) inventory in process of manufacture should be added if this item is significant in your particular type of business.

Equipment has been added because of the tendency of some Production Managers to ask for and get, for example, new, expensive, high capacity, filling, capping and labeling machines to handle both glass and plastic containers as well as wet and dry products on a high velocity basis when the capacity at the cost required by the equipment investment is not justified by the level of production needed. Production Managers tend to overequip their operations. The constant perusal of equipment catalogues and the pride of exhibiting the latest model of glistening, high capacity equipment to visiting Production Managers, student groups and other visitiors, sometimes clouds judgment. Including equipment investment in the "cost of money charge" tends to better relate production and the equipment investment required to economically meet production needs and profitability objectives.

Raw inventory and finished inventory less respective payables is a modification dictated by a tendency on the part of some production management to disregard one or the other as an investment for which production is responsible. Better raw material buying and improved production schedules result from this.

In the manufacturing field there are many variable factors involved, such as:

a. the manufacture of small, steady, high velocity consumer items or
b. the production of large pieces of equipment for which the demand is limited and the volume sporadic, so that comparisons would be meaningless.

In every instance cost of money charges tend to:

1. keep equipment investment down
2. reduce "raw" and "finished" inventories as well as inventories in process of manufacture (if applicable)
3. increase the use of suppliers' money and
4. result in improved production schedules with smooth economical operation flow.

2

SLASHING OPERATING COSTS: BOOSTING SALES VOLUME AND PROFITS WITH A NEW ELECTRONIC ORDER ENTRY SYSTEM

A new order entry system for handling routine stock replacement needs accomplished by a new system that reduces order taking time by 80%; never sleeps; is operative 24 hours a day; always prints each item on an order in warehouse sequence for economy, speed, efficiency and ease of order processing. Price strickers based on individual customer instructions as to desired "Mark up" or "Gross profit" are prepared from the same information. Quicker, more accurate "check in" and "price marking." Reduce errors; speed up order handling procedures at distribution and retail levels.

THE CHALLENGE

"Order entry" or the routine handling of telephone orders for daily replacement needs of retail customers is a growing problem in a number of distribution businesses—drug, hospital supply, grocery, oil well supply, pet supply and others.

In drug distribution (pharmaceuticals, health and beauty aids and sundries) today, a salesman writes no more than 10% of the total routine replacement need orders placed in his territory. Except under unusual circumstances, even these orders are called in to the telephone sales department for quick transmittal and to make earlier delivery schedules possible.

The growing number of incoming calls from customers to place "want book" orders (incoming calls) plus the increased telephone solicitation of suppliers seeking those orders (outgoing calls) creates an overload on even the most sophisticated telephone sales department installations, including rotary lines and other sequential call handling devices. "Busy signals," delays, lost business and disgruntled customers result. Potentially high volume business sources become fragmented.

A telephone survey, usually available from your telephone company without cost, will give you an indication of the severity of your challenge but not the remedy for it. The remedy really lies in a system that bypasses handling of routine replenishment order placements by people. A new "electronic order entry system" presently in use in more than 1,500 retail pharmacies overcomes these problems, and, in addition, provides a great many benefits for both customer and distributor—significant money and time saving benefits.

Here is an order entry system that:

- Reduces order taking time by 80%.
- Is operative 24 hours a day
- Eliminates the need for tying up qualified and expensive personnel at both the distributor and retail levels formerly required by the old manual telephone order placement procedure
- Automatically arranges the order printout by item in the sequence in which the merchandise is arranged in the warehouse. No need for "spotting," "coding" or backtracking and searching for items in the warehouse. Orders are processed more accurately, more quickly, more efficiently, and far more economically.

Better service and more profitability result. Review examples at the conclusion of this chapter.

Other benefits are:

- A shelf label for all items purchased from supplier
- Price stickers based on individual customer instructions as to gross profit or mark up desired. (This simplifies, speeds up and makes more accurate the "check in" and "price marking" procedure when orders are received by the retailer.)
- Quarterly ink color changes lets the retailer know at a glance the shelf position of all old or slow moving items; rotation of stocks is simplified. Older items in a group may

be moved up to front facings and first out movement as the product is purchased by consumers.

There are additional benefits for both customer and supplier but to pursue the entire program in depth even in summary form would require more space than this chapter permits. A lengthy, comprehensive and complete presentation would of necessity fill a large ring binder presentation manual and double the size of this book needlessly. The information can be readily developed and put in logical sequence based on the capabilities of your system. No diagrams, charts, illustrations or technical information will be presented here.

The company which develops and uses the order entry system generating the benefits outlined plus others, is nationally recognized as a pioneer and undisputed leader in the field of computer application and use in the distribution business.

The subject of the development and use of specific equipment involved in the operation is covered in separate chapters immediately following this one. It will serve the purposes of management consideration and decision making here to say simply that a combination of equipment is in use and available.

In essence, there is an order entry terminal for "in store" use. It is a simple device that uses existing telephone lines to communicate with the division computer. The in-store terminal is simple, small and designed for a busy user. It receives and stores on a cassette or solid state, digitally punched item numbers (industry code epic numbers) for each product and the quantities of each item ordered. A new order cycle starts immediately after an order is transmitted.

The "in store terminal" is not the only electronic order entry system. There are others that have many advantages. I prefer the in-store terminal because it communicates directly with the computer and does not require the use of telephone sales department personnel for order transmission.

Transmission to the distributors or the division's computer is accomplished by the use of a telephone coupler unit connected to the recorder module. A series of fail-safe devices insures accurate transmittal over regular telephone lines, as we have stated, to the division's computer which then *prints in warehouse sequence*, all of the items on the order received.

The telephone company has a device or a unit (a MODEM) which converts the sounds received from the telephone coupler unit connected to the "in store" recorder module into digital information which the division's computer understands. These numbers produce a printed item description that corresponds with that number. Price stickers are prepared from the same information. Order transmittal may be any time, day or night, seven days a week.

The pharmacy operator will usually put the telephone in the coupler unit to place his full order as he closes the store and leaves for the day, thus placing his complete order for early morning processing in the division and early or "first run" delivery the following day.

How does such a system, when installed and working efficiently, affect operating costs, sales and earnings?

Let's take a look at EXAMPLE "A" in this Chapter.

Results
Example "A" Company
Operating Costs as a Percent of Sale

| | ANNUAL | | LAST QUARTER | |
	Prior Fiscal Year	Current Fiscal Year	Prior Fiscal Year	Current Fiscal Year
Div. #1	7.8	7.0	7.3	5.7
Div. #2	8.6	6.9	6.9	6.6
Div. #3	8.1	7.3	8.6	8.0
Div. #4	9.6	8.6	9.9	8.9
Div. #5	9.9	9.7	8.6	8.1
Div. #6	9.1	8.8	10.2	8.4
Div. #7	11.0	10.5	11.1	9.4
Div. #8	11.7	10.8	10.4	8.7
Div. #9	11.0	10.0	10.5	8.8
Div. #10	10.2	10.0	8.1	7.5
Div. #11	9.0	8.3	9.5	8.5
Div. #12	10.2	9.0	8.3	8.1
Div. #13	9.1	8.4	8.9	8.5
Div. #14	9.0	9.4	10.9	9.3
Div. #15	11.5	10.8	9.3	8.5
Div. #16	10.0	9.8	9.5	8.6
Div. #17	10.4	9.5	8.4	7.0
Div. #18	9.4	8.0	7.0	6.1
Div. #19	8.1	6.6	9.2	7.9
Div. #20	9.6	8.7	8.6	7.6

Operating expenses, already low compared with the industry average of 11.52%, are trending toward further improvement during the last quarter of the current fiscal year with current fiscal operating costs generally well below the prior fiscal year.

Sales

- Increase in current fiscal year over prior fiscal year—10%.
- Increase in first quarter of new fiscal year—21%.

Pre-Tax Earnings

- Increase in current fiscal year over prior fiscal year—24%.
- Increase in first quarter of new fiscal year over prior fiscal year first quarter—70%.

These figures are so dramatic that they may raise questions of accuracy in the minds of some management people whose experience has been confined to older, more conventional methods of order solicitation and processing. The information given was taken directly from a recently audited and published statement of Example "A" company.

The interest in "electronic order entry" systems is growing and their use is becoming widespread. While time seems to be of the essence, so is caution.

To obtain a franchise on a proven workable system is more desirable than going through the trial and error entailed in originating your own "electronic order entry program." Research and development costs can run high.

Having the right program is essential—

1. Computer selection
2. Proper design and capabilities of an in-store order entry terminal and
3. Proper introduction of the service to customers.

Over and beyond these essentials, make certain that any franchise agreement you may consider requires the provision of manuals of instruction for:

1. Your "tab room," "data processing room" or "computer center"
2. Your warehouse operation
3. Your sales department.

A reputation for reliability is essential and reliability in this field depends on knowing what, where and how to do the proper thing at the right time. A thorough procedure supported by manuals of instruction is the only way to go about this. Some distributors are in a "hit or miss" position today because of haste and lack of technical knowledge.

Be especially careful of the following if you elect to handle an in-store terminal program on your own:

a. dependability of source of supply—must be well financed and have high level production capability
b. in-store terminal should be simple, with as few moving parts as possible and hence, virtually trouble-free
c. source of the terminal must have a well staffed service or repair department
d. present and future modifications of such in-store terminals must have communication capability, regardless of any modification that might evolve, with your computer system. This may appear to be a tutorial statement but be careful.
e. changes in the area of specific equipment are ceaseless and improvements continue to be made. Have your Computer Services Manager review all available equipment and arrange for a practical amount of testing before commitments are made; accept units in quantities as you are able to place them.

Other considerations are:

a. Cost of unit
b. Monthly customer service fee amount
c. Transmittal speed
d. Flexibility of unit
e. Durability of unit.

How do customers like the program?

Let's listen to what Customer "A" says:

"I have been in this program right from the start.

I had been concerned with the problems of 'checking in merchandise,' 'price marking mistakes' and 'efficient stock control.'

I knew I needed a better method of checking in merchandise that would be faster and as fool proof as possible.

I wanted an 'order entry' system that would save me time, too.

I have gained all of this plus a series of useful reports.

I find the new 'order entry' system and related services to be very reliable."

Customer "B" says simply:

"I save two and one-half man days a week by using the new 'electronic order entry system.' "

Customer "C" adds:

"My profits have increased since I began using the new 'electronic order entry system.' I like it because it helps me operate more efficiently and increases my earnings as a result."

Improvement continues to develop:

SALES

Distributor sales are continuing to reflect dramatic gains over those recorded in this chapter.

OPERATING EXPENSES

Operating costs as a percent of sales continue a highly desirable downward trend despite inflationary factors.

EARNINGS

Current pre-tax earnings are very nearly three times the earnings of the prior year, which figure itself was already beginning to reflect the results of earlier installation of a number of "in store terminals."

3

NEW PROVEN WAYS TO BOOST PRODUCTIVITY WITHOUT INCREASING CAPITAL REQUIREMENTS OR RAISING PRICES

For greater efficiencies and profits with no additional capital or change in prices, turn to your buying function; cut down lead time and reduce reserve stocks; reduce inventory investment; increase turnover with a tested new electronic ordering procedure. Customer routine stock replacement orders handled similarly reduce operating costs and increase production at the distribution level and cut ordering, receiving and pricing time in half.

THE CHALLENGE

In the routine replacement ordering process, "lead time" has been increasing or expanding continuously as a result of a number of factors which include, but are not confined to:

- slow, inefficient manual wholesaler ordering systems or procedures still in use by many distributors
- U.S. Postal Service problems—orders are in the mail too many days expanding transit time
- outmoded "order entry," "order control" and "order filling" procedures at the manufacturer level.

Increased inventory investment requirements result at all levels from the manufacturer through the distributor to the retailer. Increased inventory investment requirements, of course, tend to reduce return on investment. Excessive inventory investment generally results in increased omission rates or lower service levels which tend to reduce sales volume and profits.

Why is this so? Heavy inventory investments, one would assume, would decrease "out of stock" problems. Not so. Just the opposite is true. Excessive inventory investments result in a high omission rate. Why?

With an excessive inventory investment in relation to sales, management, interested in improving the company's R.O.I., puts pressure on the Purchasing Department to reduce inventory. Management wants results and wants it quickly. "Time is money" is an old bromide; in this case, it is literally true.

A timetable for accomplishing the desired inventory reduction is usually set up and the amount of reduction desired often is substantial, the timetable for accomplishment—brief.

"Deadlines" are set and you may have seen placards in some Purchasing Departments showing a cartoon or drawing of a lion on his back with his feet up in the air, bearing these words, "There is a dead lion in this office," and a date on which the "dead lion" expired. This is a constant visual reminder to buyers, clever, but ineffective. This is an operating challenge affecting company profits to such an extent that clever or flippant approaches or trappings are to be avoided. Inventory reduction and control are serious matters not to be taken lightly.

Purchasing Department personnel are, of course, inclined to follow the quickest, easiest procedure to accomplish inventory reduction objectives within the allotted time. What happens? Purchase quantities are reduced on the fastest selling items. Inventory investments come down noticeably and rather quickly, but omission levels or "outs" go up. With lowered "service levels" (high omission rates) sales decline and so do profits. The net result is still a relatively high inventory investment, but in the wrong items. It seems a paradox but companies with excessive inventory investments as we have stated, invariably also have an excessive number of "shorts," "outs" or "omissions."

"Lead time" is a formidable profit factor. What is "lead time"? "Lead time" is that time which expires between the date an order is placed and the date that the merchandise ordered is received.

To be more definitive, it is that time which expires between the period when an item count indicates that an ordering point has been reached, an order is prepared, sent to the manufacturer, received, processed, shipped and placed on the distributors' shelves. In reality we are talking about the time that expires in the manual preparation of an order—typing or hard copy printout, envelope addressing, folding and stuffing, mailing, the time during which the document is in transit in the postal service or United States mail (often 3 to 5 days), receipt by the manufacturer, order processing, shipping and finally the arrival, checking and shelving of the merchandise by the distributor. All of these are "lead time" factors.

What is our solution? Reduce lead time. When this is done, we reduce inventory investment requirements (increase R.O.I.) and minimize "omissions" while increasing sales and profits for the manufacturer, the distributor and the retail store as well. Where can we eliminate "lead time," lag factors that hurt profits and call for more investment in inventory at all levels? How can this be done?

SOLUTION

A wholesaler or distributor to manufacturer electronic order entry system capable of transmitting data;

1. Saves the distributor time in order preparation, folding, envelope addressing, postage and mailing time too
2. Saves time in which order is in transit in U.S. postal service or mail delivery (3 to 5 days in many instances, often longer and frequently uncertain)
3. Fixes ordering schedule to one day
4. Sees to it that data received by the manufacturer is accurate or correct as ordered
5. Does not lose time for order control or registry by manufacturer
6. Allows items ordered to be arranged in manufacturer warehouse stock sequence on order filling print out for speed in order processing
7. Assures no transposition errors on either items or quantity—no delays result
8. Permits merchandise to be picked, packed and shipped the same day or at the very latest, the day after the data is transmitted. One to three days of "lead time" are saved here. When you save lead time, you decrease safety stock levels because it is not necessary to keep as much inventory on hand due to the time it takes to receive merchandise after order placement.

Think about this———

EXAMPLE

If a distributor needs 20 pieces per week and orders every week, that distributor would need the 20 pieces that he sells plus another 20 pieces if it took one week from the time an order was mailed until the time it is received plus an additional "safety stock level" factor. Cut the lead time requirement factor in half, use the same order frequency, and inventory investment requirements are reduced by 50% on these 20 items. Project this formula throughout your inventory and your R.O.I. will reflect material improvement since in distribution operations, large and small, as well as manufacturers producing and marketing broad lines or many items, inventory often constitutes the single largest capital investment.

Nobody makes money on orders in the U.S. Postal Service or merchandise in transit;

- Not the manufacturer
- Not the wholesale distributor
- Not the retailer.

This is what "lead time," the need for reducing it and how to do it, is all about.

Here is the "how" part of the solution. How does a wholesaler or distributor get started?

First, the manufacturer must agree to get into automated order entry. There must be total commitment within the entire company if the concept is new to the manufacturer. Manufacturers are quick to recognize the inherent benefits of such a system and are not reluctant to participate. The limited few who may resist initially do not understand and have not properly evaluated the problem. They are soon converted to the new technique when they really understand the objectives to be gained and the benefits resulting from them.

Second, identify all products with existing industry code numbers.

Third, you must have some type of data processing equipment with telecommunications or have the ability to add teleprocessing to your existing equipment. If that is not possible, there are many data processing service bureaus that can provide this service. The cost is quite reasonable and you save money by using the service.

Fourth, each distributor or division of a multi-division operation must be identified by an appropriate number.

Fifth, establish communication programs used on your equipment to interface with the manufacturer's equipment.

When all of these requirements have been completed, a wholesaler is ready to start the wholesaler to manufacturer order entry system.

Careful attention must be given to a schedule for testing. Both wholesaler and manufacturer must agree upon a date that is convenient to place a telephone call that will allow both computers to establish the necessary protocol for teleprocessing. Then, they should create some test data to determine the validity of the data transmitted and received. This information should be in the industry's or trade association's standard format.

Watch out for this: Security procedures are established for identification of the persons in the data processing department authorized to place orders and a pre-established "password" or "code word" is added to the control card. This word may be changed at intervals as a further security safeguard.

Once the tests are validated for hardware, programs and security, the next and final step is validation of a test order. It is suggested that the order used for testing be a regular order that was recently mailed to the manufacturer by the wholesaler or distributor. Manufacturer's personnel are clearly instructed to carefully compare the test order transmitted with a copy of the identical order that was received in the United States mail. In order to avoid any delay in filling the regular mailed order, a photocopy should be made by the manufacturer for comparison purposes and the original order filled and processed as usual.

The comparison of the order mailed and the order teleprocessed must be checked thoroughly to determine if there are any problems so that they can be identified immediately and resolved. It should require no more than two tests of this detailed comparison to have this system installed and operating on an ongoing basis. After testing is completed, a routine schedule is established for teleprocessing of orders.

Teleprocessing plays an important role in today's technology. With the fast pace of progress in the field today, changes in processing methods are inevitable. Your responsibility is to find the best methods and means of decreasing costs. Since your biggest investment is probably in inventory, can there be a better place to start than reducing this investment and increasing inventory turnover while maintaining satisfactory and acceptable service levels to your customers?

This was the first step in a series of four developments involving manufacturers, suppliers and retailers of all sizes that have proven to be effective ways to boost productivity without increasing capital requirements or raising prices. Others now being successfully used will be outlined in detail in this chapter. (The last development became operative as this book went to press.)

Other programs followed which will be referred to as Phase II, Phase III, Phase IV and so on or they may be simply referred to as "phase" or the "system" or the "program." They are all part of the evolution of the same primary concept. These innovative concepts are profit aids to manufacturer, distributor and retailer made possible through the use of mutually helpful new procedures conceived and implemented by alert, informed, imaginative but practical distributor management.

It is not the first time in the history of American business that a customer has provided a new and startling approach to manufacturers resulting in mutually improved services and profits.

In Stanley Marcus' book *Minding the Store*,[1] Marcus describes how manufacturers were approached by Neiman-Marcus' buyers not with the customary "better price" pitch, but rather with constructive suggestions about what small and perhaps not too costly adjustments could and should be made in ladies' outer garments for better fit and more style and quality. Manufacturers were not quite prepared for this approach, never having heard it before, but they listened, responded and profited.

The same is true of the order teleprocessing procedures we have outlined and the next logical development soon follows. With electronic order entry working efficiently and well for manufacturers and suppliers, why not make the same application in handling routine stock replacement orders between retailer and wholesaler? See Chapter 2.

Such a system would require some kind of an in-store terminal for the storage and transmittal of data.

Subject "A" Company initiated an "electronic order entry system" with the first of its programs which we will refer to simply as Phase I. The "in-store" terminal was designed with emphasis being placed on simplicity.

---

[1]Stanley Marcus, *Minding the Store* (Boston: Little, Brown & Co., 1974).

THE IN-STORE TERMINAL

When an electronic order entry system is designed with only system functions in mind, a busy user will have trouble. A complicated terminal can have too many switches, too many lights, words that look like English, but make no sense. The Subject "A" Company's Phase I terminal was designed using terms common to order entry and making use of equipment as familiar as a tape recorder and a telephone. The terminal was small; it weighed nine pounds. With tape cassette storage capability, it used regular dial-up telephone lines acoustically coupled, transmitting at the rate of 200 lines per minute to the Division Receiver at any time, day or night, seven days a week.

Items ordered by product number reach the division where the digital information enters Subject "A" Company's computer. This converts the digital information to a printed customer order with the listing of each product ordered, arranged in warehouse sequence for speed, ease and accuracy of order filling.

Price stickers are also prepared based on customer designated markup or gross profit desired on each item. Thus there is a custom pricing service tailored to each customer. The sheets of price stickers are not affixed to products but attached to the invoice for customers' convenience in doing their checking and product pricing job quickly and accurately.

**WHAT DOES THE CUSTOMER PAY FOR SERVICES OF SUCH OBVIOUS
TIME AND MONEY SAVING VALUE TO HIM?**

The price to the customer:
$40.00 per month for terminal rental
$35 per month for price stickers
$75.00 Total Monthly Charge

Subject "A" Company Programs Cut:
- ordering
- receiving
- checking
- pricing time in half, in addition to improving efficiency and accuracy of pricing and checking merchandise at the store level. See Figure 3-1

A 52% timesaving at retail stated in dollars paid to trained, qualified people, adds significantly to retail operation earnings.

Later, the in-store terminal was changed to a solid state unit. It weighs only four pounds and it functions much the same as the original terminal.

Later, a new and expanded order entry stystem was made available using the Touch-Tone® telephone as a terminal or means of order input. For those customers who do not want the advantages of portability or storage capability it is a simple and effective communications device for order placement. The retailer simply writes an item number from the shelf label or from the price sticker affixed to the product on a pad and keys it into the

COMPARISON OF TIME FACTOR IN ELECTRONIC AND MANUAL ORDER PLACEMENT AND PRICING

Phase Cuts Ordering, Receiving and Pricing Time in Half!

TIME SPENT ORDERING:

Ordering 23 lines (165 pieces over telephone).

Ordering 23 lines (165 pieces over phone with PHASE Terminal).

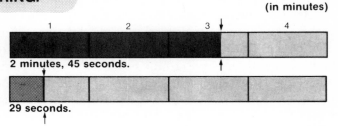

RECEIVING AND PRICING:

Receiving and pricing 165 pieces in your store, present method.

Receiving and pricing 165 pieces in your store using PHASE.

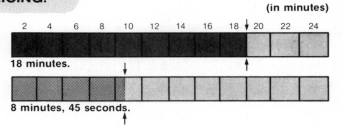

TOTAL TIME SPENT:

Ordering, receiving and pricing 23 lines (165 pieces) in your store with present method.

Ordering, receiving and pricing 23 lines (165 pieces) in your store, using PHASE.

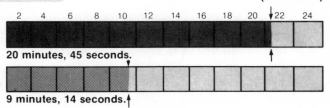

ACTUAL TIME SAVINGS WITH PHASE 52%

Figure 3-1

Comparison of Time Factor in Electronic and Manual Order Placement and Pricing

49

Touch-Tone telephone installed in the retailer's location. The Touch-Tone telephone averages 10 to 14 lines per minute and the data is transmitted to Subject "A" Company's computer. See Figures 3-2 ® and 3-3.

The Touch-Tone telephone becomes the in-store terminal device. Small, inexpensive and with limitations to be sure, it is still a vast improvement over calling in an order personally. Expanded and significant use by manufacturer's representatives of the Touch-Tone telephone for placement of "turnover orders" was conceived through the use of toll free "800" numbers and a Touch-Tone telephone anywhere (hotel room, office or store) became a terminal device for order placement use. More on this later.

Each key pressed on a Touch-Tone telephone generates two audible tones. One tone indicates the row the button is in and the other tone indicates the column in which it is located. These tones are carried over the telephone lines and interpreted by a modem which changes the tones to a digit representing the key that was pressed. This digital system data is then passed to the Subject "A" Company computer through an interface cable. The computer system used has stored within it the necessary computer programs. These programs direct the system to perform various functions with the data that has been teleprocessed by way of the telephone lines and modems. In the case of order entry, the digital information is examined for validity and the product code is verified to be correct by means of the modulus 10 check digit. After the system verifies the quantity being ordered, an audible response is returned to the user via the telephone by emitting digital information which is translated into words which go through the interface cable to the modem to the telephone line and ultimately, present themselves as audible words to the user of the telephone handset.

After the system has accepted the information, the program checks to see on which of the telephone lines the data came. The programs thus keep track of which customer is using a specific line at any given time. The program knows where to store the information it has just received.

We have now covered in chronological order, a rather comprehensive review of the evolution of terminal and/or computer use at retail, wholesaler and manufacturer levels of operation.

The names, numbers, makes and models of all equipment and their interfacings are known but we have refrained from mentioning them for these reasons:

a. Change is ceaseless, improvements are constant in the field of electronic technology and obsolescence comes quickly.

b. The availability of smaller, more flexible and greater capacity hardware at lower costs has to be accepted as a certainty.

c. To set out the names and numbers of equipment in use might tend to encourage abandonment of equipment already in use which could possibly be easily and readily adapted to meet the capabilities available in a specific piece of equipment reported as being used.

d. Selection of hardware should properly be the responsibility of management after careful and thorough study of needs as well as equipment capacity and flexibility.

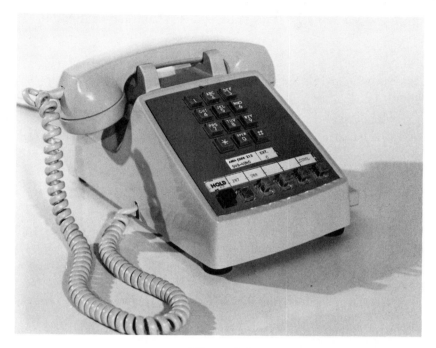

Figure 3-2

Touch-Tone Telephone Used as a Computer Terminal

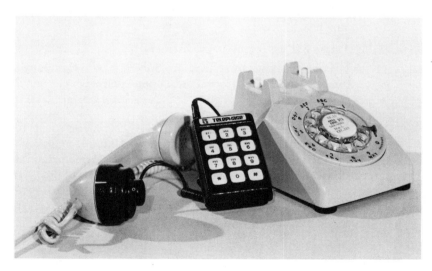

Figure 3-3

Touch-Tone Telephone With Dial Telephone Adapter

See Figure 3-4, a copy of the Subject "A" Company's Retailer Participation Agreement.

I hereby agree to participate in Subject "A" Company's [name] program under the following conditions:

I. Subject "A" Company will pay for the installation of a Touch-Tone® Telephone in my store ....

    (a) It is understood that all orders transmitted via Touch-Tone® will be toll free.

    (b) It is understood that the regular monthly phone charges for my Touch-Tone® Telephone will be my responsibility.

II. Subject "A" Company will pay for the installation of an Adjunct Unit to my present rotary dial telephone in my store ....

    (a) It is understood that all orders transmitted via the Touch-Tone® Adjunct will be toll free.

    (b) It is understood that the regular monthly charges for the Touch-Tone® Adjunct will be my responsibility.

III. I agree to participate in the [name] program through the use of Subject "A" Company's [name] Terminal ....

    (a) It is understood that all orders transmitted via the [name] Terminal will be toll free.

    (b) It is understood that I will pay $75.00 plus sales tax for the [name] Terminal.

        (1) Please bill me on my next statement ....

        (2) I agree to pay by check to Subject "A" Company's Customer Marketing Consultant upon delivery of my [name] Terminal ....

    (c) My [name] Terminal number is _____.

IV. I agree to participate in Subject "A" Company's Unlimited Custom Pricing program at the standard charge of $35.00 per month. I understand that this program provides individual retail prices on my selection of products, complete file maintenance, self-maintaining or fixed retail prices, permanent shelf labels, bi-monthly maintenance of labels and all necessary material required ....

Figure 3-4

Subject "A" Company
U.S.A.
Retailer Participation Agreement

I agree to receive the [name] Management Report at the charge of $25.00 per month. I understand that my [name] Management Report will be maintained monthly and provided quarterly ....

Store Name _____

Address/City _____

Owner/Manager _____

Date _____

Subject "A" Company

Division Manager

Date

Customer Marketing Consultant

Figure 3-4 (continued)

Subject "A" Company

U.S.A.

Retailer Participation Agreement

NEW DEVELOPMENTS

Currently, a new in-store terminal weighing only two pounds has been developed. This terminal, called Phase IV, is compact—3½ inches by 8 inches. It has the capacity to store 200 to 400 items in a solid state storage medium with speeds of 200 items per minute up to 600 items per minute with the biggest enhancement. It is capable of reading (Universal Product Code) Bar Coding from either shelf labels or actual items that have the code printed on them, by means of a built-in optical scanner.

Manual entry of product description numbers are no longer necessary. And think of the speed with which physical inventories can now be taken and priced!

Retailer benefits

- retailer price stickers (custom prepared, based on customer pricing policy)
- manufacturer price change information
- Pharmacy Management Reports.

Distributor benefits

- Orders received 24 hours a day, 7 days a week
- Order processing time is 150% faster.

For every 100 lines per hour previously picked, the picker can now pick 250 lines per hour.

- Faster delivery
- Significant reduction of claim and credit memoranda
- Bypass order taker (eliminates manual error)
- Sales Costs decline since salesmen can handle more customers
- Sales increase
- Number of items or lines per order double
- Increases average line extension
- Direct vendor is placed at a disadvantage. Retailer prefers distributor as a source because of convenience factors and additional benefits that aid in inventory control at the retail level.

Before concluding this chapter, let's return for a moment to the manufacturer. Many manufacturers have field representatives who write orders and turn them over to a wholesaler or distributor of the retailer's choice for handling, hence the term "turnover order."

Getting "turnover orders" to distributors for prompt processing and early delivery has for years been a persistent and aggravating challenge for manufacturers' representatives. The new electronic order entry terminal concept has the ingredients of a solution. The following letter (Figure 3-5) was mailed to all major suppliers by Subject "A" Company:

TO OUR SUPPLIER'S SALES REPRESENTATIVE:

Welcome to (PHASE)!

We at Subject "A" Company recognize the vital role you play in the pharmacies we service. Your turnover orders are vitally important to us, to you and your company.

(PHASE) has been designed specifically for you. It enables you to quickly and conveniently place all of your turnover orders through Subject "A" Company's distribution center. And, you can do this from any Touch-Tone® telephone anywhere in the United States, twenty four hours a day, seven days a week through our toll free number NATIONWIDE (800) _____. In addition, you can be sure that your order will be accurately filled and shipped with our next delivery to the customer. All (PHASE) turnover orders will receive top priority.

With the advent of electronic order entry, some systems are so designed that they discourage or even preclude manufacturer's turnover orders from being easily integrated into the system. This is to the customer's disadvantage as well as to yours. With Subject

Figure 3-5

THE SUBJECT "A" COMPANY
U.S.A.

"A" Company's (PHASE) system, we welcome your turnover orders. You may enter them for any of your customers and they will receive the same benefits as though they were processed through the system by the customer. Whether he is on (PHASE) or not makes no difference.

Electronic order entry is a new, more efficient method of doing business, and we at Subject "A" Company are anxious to share these benefits with you. We know that (PHASE) will enable you to save time and money while we both better serve the customer.

Please feel free to contact any of our distribution centers for further information about (PHASE).

Cordially,

SUBJECT "A" COMPANY

John Doe, President

Figure 3-5 (continued)
The Subject "A" Company
U.S.A.

How was the invitation to participate in this program received by manufacturers? Here are the responses to that letter:

Manufacturer No. 1

Congratulations on the development and forthcoming inauguration of (PHASE). This is an exciting innovation in the processing of turnover orders. All of us are eager to cooperate with you in getting the system operative and properly used on the inauguration date.

Manufacturer No. 2

Thank you for your recent letter regarding (PHASE). It is a fascinating idea and one which will be of tremendous service to retailers, as well as manufacturers' representatives.

Manufacturer No. 3

I want to extend my personal congratulations to you and your people for your innovative (PHASE) program. Surely you must be proud of the many original adaptations which you have made of computers and data processing, and the progress they have made to our industry.

We at (Manufacturer No. 3) not only congratulate you, but will look forward to cooperating with (PHASE) to the full extent of our capability.

Manufacturer No. 4

Congratulations on your new electronic order entry system . . . (PHASE). It truly reflects creative and innovative thinking and based on your description, it should ultimately provide for a faster, more efficient method of processing turnover orders when pharmacists designate Subject "A" Company as their supplier.

I heartily agree that the concept of electronic order entry has many merits. Certainly, it will help speed new product and deal stocking at the pharmacy level and will reduce out-of-stock situations on established products. Also, equally important is the potential savings in our representatives handling time of turnover orders.

Manufacturer No. 5

Your new (PHASE) service represents a giant step forward and will assuredly result in greater cooperation and productivity between suppliers and your organization.

Manufacturer No. 6

This will acknowledge your letter concerning the exciting new (PHASE) program you have inaugurated for key suppliers. The program is a most imaginative innovation. The results should be mutually beneficial to the manufacturer as well as the wholesaler.

The manufacturer of course, can get his turnover orders quickly and accurately filled, which will also benefit (your company) since it has been often reported by our men that some of our turnover orders are never filled.

I should like to offer my congratulations to you on this exciting breakthrough.

Manufacturer No. 7

Congratulations to you and to (your company) on another new innovation directed toward improving our sales and service of the retail trade. The new (PHASE) system sounds exciting, modern and right on target.

We will provide full information on the (PHASE) system to all salesmen who cover areas serviced by (your company).

Manufacturer No. 8

We at (Manufacturer No. 8) especially those in the Sales area, are just as excited about the new (PHASE) program as you are. This innovative step in drug wholesaling should go a long way toward increasing the productivity of our sales force. It will also, due to the rapid handling of turnover orders, reduce the out-of-stocks on our products, something we are always striving to do.

Manufacturer No. 9

It certainly appears that your next innovative (PHASE) system offers significant benefits to both of our organizations, and we at (Manufacturer No. 9) are enthusiastic about its possibilities.

Thank you for informing us of (PHASE). We appreciate your progressive posture in the service wholesale industry and wish you every success with your unique new system.

Manufacturer No. 10

Thank you for informing us of your new (PHASE) system. It is certainly unique and a great breakthrough in our industry.

I have informed our Regional Managers of the (PHASE) program and I assure you that we will utilize it in turnover orders for your Company.

Manufacturer No. 11

The new system, (PHASE), that you are implementing sounds very exciting as well as innovative. I am certain it will be beneficial to you, your customers, and your key suppliers.

A bulletin announcing (PHASE) will be sent to all field sales personnel along with the (PHASE) cards, as soon as they are received.

Manufacturer No. 12

Let me tell you that this is really a breakthrough and will prove extremely valuable for all of us. I will be getting the mechanics squared away covering those major vendors we represent, but I did want to drop you a note and wish you success in this new venture. Fighting paperwork and mail deliveries for as long as I have (PHASE) at least for our turnover orders, is nothing short of a miracle.

Manufacturer No. 13

You've done it again! I was most excited to read about the new (PHASE) system. We are beginning to turn the wheels to incorporate a field sales procedure that will enable us to capitalize on your program.

I'm recommending a special turnover order form be considered so that turnover orders can be organized in a manner to efficiently use (PHASE).

I am recommending our Sales and Marketing Departments take advantage of the uniqueness of (PHASE) by developing a special promotional drive that will (a) increase our volume through your company and (b) familiarize our salesmen with the advantages of your (PHASE) system.

Manufacturer No. 14

Thank you very much for your letter describing your new service. It would appear that this new innovative system has many exciting possibilities, both for you as a wholesaler and for the manufacturers whose prime concern is adequate distribution.

Manufacturer No. 15

I read with interest your letter concerning your new (PHASE) system. Obviously, we should be delighted to participate in your program. You are always staying a few jumps ahead of the pack. It does sound like a very exciting significant step in handling retail calls.

Manufacturer No. 16

This is a very inventive approach, and we congratulate you on providing what appears to be a very time saving system for sales use in ordering our products.

Manufacturer No. 17

Your new (PHASE) is a tremendous idea and you will have our wholehearted support.

Manufacturer No. 18

I share your enthusiasm for the new (PHASE) service described in your leter, and the (Manufacturer No. 18) sales force will cooperate in every respect.

Manufacturer No. 19

Congratulations on your new (PHASE) program. It is indeed an innovative system and one that should provide a nice competitive edge for you.

Manufacturer No. 20

We are delighted that you have included (Manufacturer No. 20) and I must congratulate you and your organization on this tremendous step forward. It really represents a tremendous breakthrough.

Manufacturer No. 21

I was delighted to hear about the new (PHASE) program. Both you and I can recall, when not too many years ago, the use of computers was virtually restricted to accounting and billing functions. It comes as no surprise to me that the first practical application of this technological tool to the manufacturers sales operation comes from the leadership of your company.

Manufacturer No. 22

(Manufacturer No. 22) is happy to participate in your new (PHASE) program and we congratulate your company for taking such an innovative approach to the servicing of the retail pharmacies throughout the country.

We wish your company complete success with the new (PHASE) system and look forward to the continuous development of programs that will improve the selling and servicing of the retail drug trade.

Manufacturer No. 23

We have acknowledged receipt of all the new (PHASE) material and we have distributed the material to our sales representatives servicing your division.

1984 got here a little soon, but believe me this is quite an advancement in the art and it will be most interesting to see it work.

Manufacturer No. 24

The concept is novel, very forward looking and our sales people tell us it is the first time such a thorough system has come to our attention.

You and your organization may be sure that we at (Manufacturer No. 24) are most anxious to cooperate and the appropriate people have been alerted to your new and unique program.

Manufacturer No. 25

When we saw your letter and brochure regarding your company's new (PHASE) program we were very enthusiastic about it. I immediately placed a phone call to *** complimenting him on the excellent and unique idea your company has with this program. It has got to be one of the finest opportunities that we manufacturers have had to quickly, accuratley and economically transmit our mutual customers' turnover orders directly to your central computer.

Manufacturer No. 26

*** forwarded your letter of *** to me for reply. We agree that you indeed should be excited about your new (PHASE) program. It certainly is a significant step forward for everyone.

Manufacturer No. 27

First I want to congratulate all of you at your company for the innovative program (PHASE), and I want to assure you that Manufacturer No. 27 will give you 100 percent cooperation in those areas in the U.S. serviced by your divisions. I have discussed this with our Marketing group, and if they have any questions, they will get in touch with ***.

You have read the words; let's look at the figures. They demonstrate impressively the success of the (PHASE) program.

Volume Increase by Manufacturer Since Inauguration of Program

Manufacturer	Percentage
Manufacturer #1	24% +
Manufacturer #2	43% +
Manufacturer #3	29% +
Manufacturer #4	88% +
Manufacturer #5	39% +
Manufacturer #6	25% +
Manufacturer #7	43% +
Manufacturer #8	5% +
Manufacturer #9	95% +
Manufacturer #10	5% +
Manufacturer #11	16% +
Manufacturer #12	N.A.
Manufacturer #13	31% +
Manufacturer #14	50% +
Manufacturer #15	42% +
Manufacturer #16	65% +
Manufacturer #17	11% +
Manufacturer #18	43% +
Manufacturer #19	15% +
Manufacturer #20	7% +
Manufacturer #21	N.A.
Manufacturer #22	N.A.

Manufacturer	*Percentage*
Manufacturer #23	20% +
Manufacturer #24	515% +
Manufacturer #25	N.A.
Manufacturer #26	N.A.
Manufacturer #27	50% +

These increases in purchases did not result in increases in inventory investment. Sell-through was accelerated. These are early tabulations in the life of the program. Subsequent increased percentages have grown appreciably.

In mass retailing the objective for some years has been to handle the buying function, especially the reorder part of buying, through the use of statistical formula fed into an electronic order entry system. Such a system was developed and in use as early as 1969 in placing routine replenishment stock orders for super markets. Usually the application was to replace shelf stock from the warehouse. It is believed to be one of the earliest practical applications of such a system, if not the first one. By today's standards, the equipment and procedures then in use were, for the most part, cumbersome, unwieldy and have long since been replaced by more modern, more useful hardware and more refined programs and procedures.

It was a start—not an auspicious one—but a start. Like the super market industry itself, experimentation has become innovation.

The drug distribution business used a somewhat different approach and expanded and proliferated its programs quite rapidly, involving both sources of supply and customers, because of the need as well as the availability, of more economical, more sophisticated equipment and programming. Electronic order entry was reportedly not the primary objective of the supermarket application of routine stock replacement. In the drug industry that was, and is, the primary objective, starting with the supplier and then making the application to the handling of customer orders as well. Other benefits developed relating to inventory control, management reports and other factors are simply collateral benefits.

In summary here are the developments. They are new, but tested with successful results:

MANUFACTURER

1. An electronic order entry system has been developed and established by a distributor or wholesaler to reduce lead time on orders placed with major suppliers and then expanded to suppliers or manufacturers of lesser importance, who wanted to participate in the program.

2. A program whereby the Touch-Tone® telephone or an adapter with a Touch-Tone® key board for use where only dial telephone equipment is available gives manufacturer sales representatives a terminal that can be used anywhere for placing "turnover orders" with a distributor for prompt processing and delivery of items ordered.

See manufacturer responses given in preceding paragraphs of this chapter.

DISTRIBUTOR

Subject "A" Company's programs 1, 2, 3 and 4 made it increasingly convenient for the retailer to place orders through a series of in-store terminals. An inventory management system, retail price stickers, permanent stock control shelf labels and a series of useful custom management reports were by-products of the electronic order entry terminals. Customer preference and stronger, better managed stores for more profitability helped expand and increase wholesaler sales volume to viable, profitable stores.

RETAILER

A series of order entry systems ranging from the first in store terminal to the Touch-Tone telephone used as an order terminal, have compacted ordering, receiving and pricing time. Other benefits in the way of a variety of useful management reports exist.

Here then are a proven number of new ways to boost productivity without increasing capital requirements or raising prices regardless of the size of your business or whether you are a manufacturer, wholesaler, distributor or retailer.

RESULTS

Inventory Turnover

Prior	Now
7½ turns per year	8.8 turns per year

One and one-third more turns a year gives a wholesaler a substantial gross profit increase in dollars based on inventory investment.

This is what return on investment is all about.

Comparative Omission Rates
(All Divisions)

Prior	Now
4.45% of Sales	3.5% of Sales

A decrease in omission rates of .95%, almost 1% improvement made a significant contribution to sales and profit increases.

SALES

Sales increase 29.8%, almost a 30% increase, of which 1% is made up of lowered omission rates.

In summary:

- inventories have been reduced
- inventory turnover has been significantly increased
- omission rates have been lowered
- sales volume has increased.

You are well on your way towards reaching your goal—more profit from less money invested.

4

NEW TECHNIQUES IN ORDER ENTRY AND INFORMATION RETRIEVAL SYSTEMS

How to substantially reduce personnel through application of the in-store terminal device system and maximize use of your own computer capability.

THE CHALLENGE

SUBJECT COMPANY "A" set up a program to automate the order entry process. This chapter outlines that development.

There are basically three procedures for handling routine order entry. All of them work but with varying degrees of efficiency.

1. The oldest procedure, and the one still most widely used despite its inefficiencies and constantly increasing costs, is the person-to-person system of order placement. This is the daily (sometimes more frequent) customer to Telephone Sales Department manual telephone call procedure.

DISADVANTAGES

A. It is slow

B. It is error prone

C. It is expensive in that it ties up qualified personnel who could devote time more productively at both retail and wholesale levels

D. Items are written in random order and not in warehouse sequence which adds to order filling costs.

2. The in-store terminal to Telephone Sales Department order placement procedure.

DISADVANTAGES

A. Orders still must go through the Telephone Sales Department and this involves people; there is possible high error frequency and Telephone Sales Department overload at peak order placement hours. Only retailer personnel has been freed to perform other duties; the wholesaler is still coping manually with the routine order entry procedure.

3. The third procedure is to provide a reliable in-store terminal to communicate directly with the wholesaler's or the distributor's computer.

ADVANTAGES

A. Personnel at retail and wholesale are freed to perform other duties

B. Machines communicate more efficiently—more rapidly

C. Items on an order are arranged in warehouse sequence for economy, ease and speed of order filling.

D. Important information retrieval possibilities exist for use in the preparation of a series of valuable management reports including inventory control.

In reviewing the development of the "in-store terminal" by Subject Company "A," we find that the system made use of two order entry devices—Data Acquisition Recording Terminal #1 and Data Acquisition Recording Terminal #2. Both of these devices perform approximately the same functions:

- Keyboard entry of product codes and quantities
- Visible display of information
- Error detection of improper product codes
- Storage of products and quantities ordered
- Transmission of order information to a central site by way of the telephone at medium speeds (approximately 200 products per minute).

While both of these units were satisfactory, they had some definite shortcomings:

- Unit #1 weighed about 10 pounds. This curtailed its portability somewhat.

- Unit #1 employed the use of a cassette recorder and, being a mechanical device, it required more servicing than was desirable.
- Unit #1 allowed input only from its own keyboard. There were no auxiliary devices to enable reading machine-readable codes.
- *Unit #2 used a very small visual display. This forced the user to erase his order before entering a new order. Thus, there was no ability to look back at a previous order to check if a product was already ordered.*
- Unit #2 did not allow for directly coupling its transmission unit to the telephone lines in areas where acoustic coupling was unacceptable.

In summary, these units were designed and manufactured with the "state of the art" techniques available in the early 1970's. Knowing full well how quickly the technology changes, Subject Company "A" set out to develop the order entry terminal of tomorrow. This unit will be referred to simply as UNIT #3. The search showed that other people had merely refined the same technology that was already in use in the existing equipment. No one was producing, nor were they planning to produce, any terminal that made use of the fantastic breakthroughs in today's proven technology.

Subject Company "A"'s search had defined the terminal that would answer the system requirements of tomorrow. With these specifications in hand they embarked on a project which required a substantial commitment of time and money.

After reviewing the capabilities of numerous manufacturers, one was selected that had the necessary prime ingredients for a successful venture. These were:

1. Financial strength
2. Manufacturing capabilities
3. High production capacity
4. Extensive and competent servicing force

The project was carried to completion. After twelve months of careful research and development, the UNIT #3 project yielded its fruit.

This new information entry terminal UNIT#3 is the result of a delicate interweaving of electronic and human engineering assembled in a totally rugged and durable modern package. Its features seem to answer all, or most, of today's and tomorrow's questions.

Here is a description of the new UNIT#3 terminal:

- Lightweight — slightly over 2 pounds
- Compact — 8 inches high x 3-3/4 inches wide x 1-1/2 inches deep (can be carried in a salesman's coat pocket or portfolio)
- Self-contained - no wires to attach batteries, storage or auxiliary equipment.

The terminal is a modular construction of five subsystem parts:

1. *The Keyboard* for manual information entry.
2. *The Scanner* for entering information automatically by scanning a machine-readable Bar Code.

3. *The Display* for visually showing the user that he has entered information, or for reviewing information previously entered.
4. *The Controller* for guiding and checking the validity of each function that the terminal and user perform.
5. *The Memory/Power Pack* for storing the information entered and supplying power to the terminal.

The terminal is therefore a special purpose micro-computer. Its inputs are the keyboard and scanner; its output is the display. It incorporates a random access memory; it uses a micro-processor as its controller.

The most significant advantages of the terminal are:

1. The bar-code scanner which is built directly into the handset enables the unit to "read" Universal Product Codes (UPC), versions A and E. This is the same code that you see on almost all of the grocery store items you buy. By labeling the shelves of stores with this type of bar-code, order entry time for preparing the order is reduced by half. The scanner can read from the product itself or from a label on the shelf.
2. The memory of the unit is a solid state memory—it has no moving parts to wear out. But even more significant—the memory is removable! Even after removing the memory, the information contained in it is still useable and can be held for future use. (This is referred to as a non-volatile memory.) The unit can store from 400 to 800 products to be ordered.
3. The controller allows a user to search through memory in two ways:
   • You may look for a specific product, or
   • You may "browse" through memory to review everything you have entered.

In addition to these major advantages, the following are other significant features:

• All product codes are validated - whether entered from the keyboard or the scanner.
• All detected errors are indicated by a visual and audible alarm.
• Warning and Guidance indicators flash to indicate Low Battery, Unit in Search Mode, Memory Storage Full, Quantity Entry Expected.
• The display uses a large size digit and two separate lines to separate product code, status indications and quantity information. This assures clarity.
• At any time the unit can display exactly how much room remains in its memory.
•cThe case is made of molded contoured Lexan.® This material is virtually breakproof.
• The electronics are shock mounted so that an occasional fall will not cause the unit to malfunction.

The only other piece of equipment involved in getting the order entry information from the new UNIT#3 terminal to the order receiving point is the communication module.

This unit is also a micro-processor controlled device. It serves three functions:

1. It recharges the batteries in the Memory/Power Pack.

2. It allows the user to operate his new terminal on 120 volt AC power (wall outlet power) in a stationary mode.
3. It transmits order information over the telephone line.

The Communication Module will "listen" to the receiving computer and if it "says" that the order was receiving correctly, the Communication Module lights up a green indicator to show the user that everything was correct. Otherwise a red indicator is turned on to show that the order must be retransmitted.

The entire terminal has been designed to fit into the human environment in which it will be used. Its complete use of space-age electronics and technology make it the most rugged and reliable device of its type ever manufactured. Its human engineering makes it the easiest and most pleasant device to use.

RESULTS

1. Larger, more accurately filled orders
2. Expense levels dropped to between 5% and 8%, compared to 9-1/2% to 12% levels for the industry generally
3. Profits increased materially.

Simply put, without the computer and a reliable in-store terminal, operating expense levels will remain too high for profitability in today's business environment.

Benefiting from the past experimentation of others, a feasibility study of the application of this new technology in your business will take into account these significant factors:

1. The availability of more refined, more reliable, trouble free, in-store terminals
2. The cost of the terminals decided upon and monthly rental or use charge to be made to customers
3. The cost or monthly rental of such a computer system and comparative costs with that of existing convention methods
4. The most suitable and compatible computer installation in your plant
5. Programming
6. Timetable for initiation, development, completion, presentation to customers and/or suppliers.

The use of an electronic order entry system has an impressive historical record of known favorable results.

While this chapter has been given the title "New Techniques in Order Entry and Information Retrieval Systems," the micro-computer (UNIT #3), and illustrations of its predecessors are shown on the following pages as well as the Touch-Tone® telephone adapter for dial telephone installations.

There are also illustrations of the micro-computer for in-store use made available as this book goes to press. The unit is operative as of the release date of this book. You have been given a word description of it. See Figures 4-1 through 4-3A.

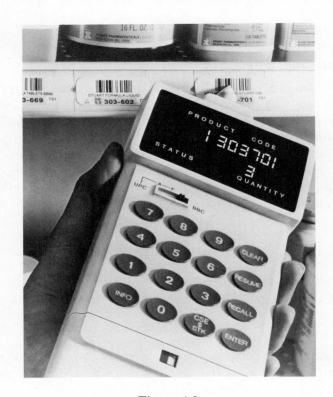

Figure 4-1

Hand Held Micro-Computer Module

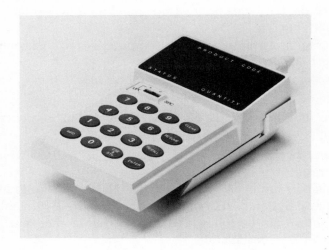

Figure 4-1A

Micro-Computer Module

68

Figure 4-2

Memory Pack

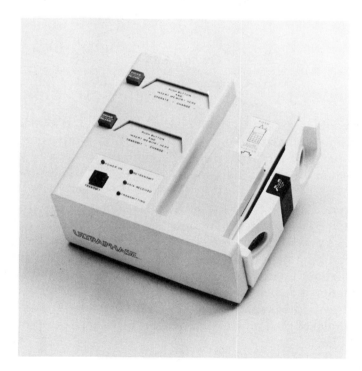

Figure 4-3

Service Module

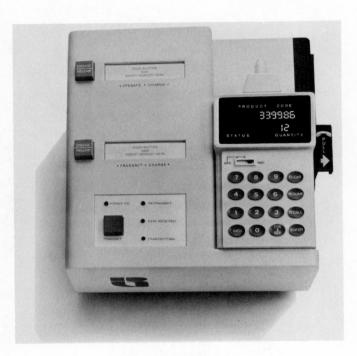

Figure 4-3A

Micro-Computer and Service Module

You will be reading a great deal about new micro-computers in many trade journals in the years just ahead. You have had one, the first really innovative one described in some detail in this chapter. It is a reliable piece of equipment.

With innovation, as with investments, "what everybody knows is not worth knowing."

The micro-computer functions efficiently in two important areas of communications:

1. Units #1 and 2 provide an instant ordering system that enables both retailers and distributors to place orders around the clock, seven days a week, inexpensively.

2. Unit #3 is an information retrieval system that gives pharmacists instant access to basic information about products, prices, marketing and merchandising. A voluminous amount of information is dispensed. Subject Company "A" calls the process by which this information is dispensed Microform,® although it is generally known as Microfiche.® Microform® (Microfiche®) is similar to microfilm, except that it is reproduced in sheet film instead of rolled film.

More specifically, information is furnished by magnetic computer tape into a system which condenses the information on a sheet of film. One sheet contains as much information as hundreds of pages of standard size paper. *For example, the contents of approximately 500 catalog size pages can be reproduced on a single sheet of 4 inch by 6 inch microfilm.*

To read the data, the pharmacist places this sheet of film on a viewer which magnifies the contents to normal page size. The microfilm has an index for quick reference as well as grids or frames. In Unit #3, there are two strips of the 4" x 6" microform or film. One carries pricing and product data, the other management and merchandising information.

The pricing/product Microform,® updated every two weeks, is divided into eight sections and includes the following information:

- a complete list of products available from any Subject Company "A" warehouse or division
- their cost to the retailer
- DEA classification
- product price or size changes
- prepack deals
- discontinued items
- return goods policies of 200 top Rx and OTC drug manufacturers
- free goods on deals and other product information.

The management/merchandising microform, updated monthly, includes such information as:

- photos of manufacturers' selling sheets on deals, etc.
- the names of products recalled by manufacturers
- upcoming sales promotion information
- price change lists
- other services.

All told, the UNIT #3 program reduces 1,000 pages of information to two microforms occupying less than one square foot of prescription department space, and in so doing, maintains all pertinent reference material at a central location in easy reference form. The cost to retailers is $10.00 to $40.00 a month, including the viewer. The exact cost depends upon the number of options the pharmacist selects, such as using microform for prescription records or for patient profiles, etc.

This then is the order entry terminal of tomorrow, today. It is illustrated in Figures 4-4 through 4-4B.

In this text, a number of the successful modern corporate management techniques outlined involve the use of a computer system to:

1. reduce operating costs
2. reduce capital investment requirements
3. simplify and make more efficient a number of operations functions
4. reduce the number of people required to handle these functions.

These concepts are still new enough so that many Chief Executive Officers who attempt to use them are sure to run into conceptual, application and/or operational difficulties unless the C.E.O., himself, has a good working knowledge of available hardware,

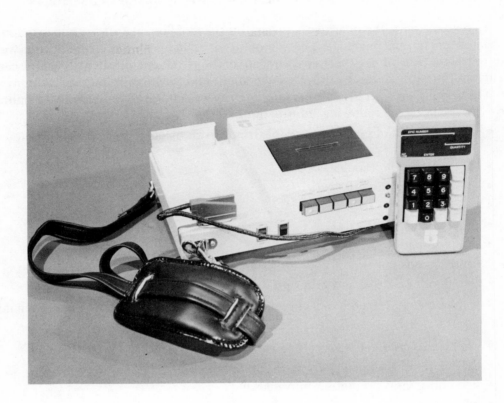

Figure 4-4

Recorder Module

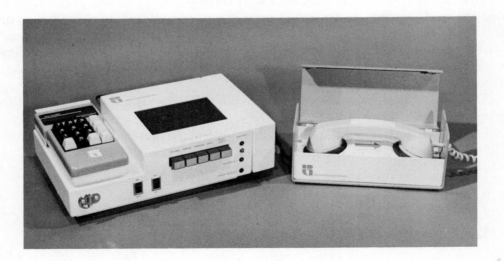

Figure 4-4A

Telephone Coupler Unit

72

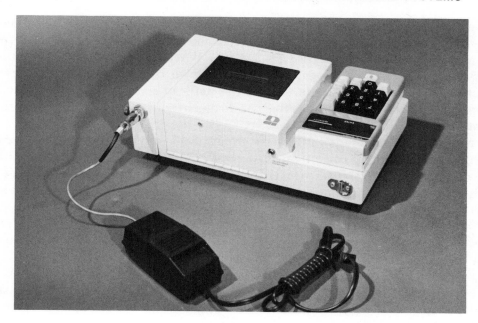

Figure 4-4B

Power Pack and Telephone Coupler Connector

modification possibilities and compatability features as well as a thorough understanding of programs that must be prepared and used properly for the specific results he wants. He must also know something about the present "state of the arts" in the computer field as well as what new developments, if applied properly, would provide his company with a competitive edge or advantage. This is a heavy and continuing responsibility. Initiative and imagination are as essential to the green edge of growth and to success in this area as in other management endeavors.

The "computer" is by no means the answer to all of your operational and cost control problems. Computers can be and are used to great advantage but this versatile device does present some pitfalls to the unwary user. Waste, needless expense and under-utilization of equipment can rob you of any real benefits.

EXAMPLE

Management is sometimes quick to state, "my operations are computerized" and then with some pride name the specific computer, usually a large one with a wide range of capabilities. How is the computer used? It is used to:

a. write payroll checks
b. handle accounts payable
c. handle accounts receivable
d. prepare aged-analysis of accounts
e. maintain the general ledger.

These elementary uses sum up the total application of a computer identical to that used to successfully send the astronauts to the moon and then return them back to earth. Management is using it only to "fly a kite." What a waste of capability this is! Management's concept of the capabilities of his own computer system is sometimes woefully inadequate. He has reduced it to the status of a very expensive bookkeeping machine while paying for something that can do much more and would if put to work with the proper programs.

The major manufacturers in the electronics field provide seminars, memoranda, pamphlets and books that cogently explain their hardware functions and capabilities as well as outline programs (software) that the equipment can handle. Research and development is ceaseless and continuing access to all the information that a C.E.O. can get on this subject is desirable.

Start a file of this material and encourage your Data Processing Department Manager to route copies of all new material to you. Read it and set aside some time each week or each month for discussions and updating.

During the Bicentennial Year, we spent a lot of time looking back but in business none of the answers are to be found in reviewing the way things have been done in the past. We are moving much too swiftly for that. Successful management tactics and procedures are being hammered out today in an atmosphere that was never more competitive, never more intolerant of error; nor have the stakes ever been so high.

It should be stated again in concluding this chapter, that the advantage of an electronic order entry system that connects the in-store terminal directly with the supplier's computer has a primary advantage that other systems with other benefits do not have, and that is that the need no longer exists to send every routine replacement order through an overloaded telephone sales department with human error tendencies that increase with the work load. The in-store terminal avoids this operation bottleneck.

Reviewing the **Results** sections provided at the conclusion of each of the chapters of this book will disclose how much improvement may be traced to the simple improvement of order entry techniques. A lot of what you do better and more profitably starts here.

PART II
OPERATIONS

Three New Procedures That Cut Operating Costs in Half and Keep Them There

5

THE RED CARD SYSTEM: IDENTIFYING AND ELIMINATING NON-MOVING ITEMS FROM STOCK

How to pinpoint and scrap dead weight in inventory. Procedures to release inventory dollars tied up in non-movers, effective in both manual and computerized systems if proper information is immediately fed into your computer. The red-card system assures precise input.

THE CHALLENGE

Excessive inventory investment is usually found in those items in which there is no movement at all rather than in too much inventory of any item moving slowly, but with reasonable regularity.

Computer inventory control systems are not without problems. In the early stages of implementation, inventories sometimes tend to increase substantially and it is not unusual to experience significant temporary increases in omission rates. The shortcomings of manual (buyer-stock card) systems are too well known to enumerate here and have resulted in a growing trend to rely on computer programs for more efficient buying and inventory control.

Whether your company is on computerized buying, is still on the buyer-stock card system, or in a period of transition, you would benefit from the use of a new technique to identify and eliminate non-moving items. It is manual, visual, simple to install and operate, and it works. I call it the Red Card System.

The problem is to identify dead items in stock.

Here is the procedure:

Simply place a blank red IBM card in front of the deck of IBM cards in the IBM card bin located adjacent to each item in the warehouse if you are on IBM billing. Order clerks or pickers are instructed to pull the red card, tear it up and throw it away, then pull the billing card when one or more pieces of any item in stock is filled on an order. Quantity is not important. What we are looking for is any movement at all—even one piece.

Thirty or sixty days after placing the red IBM cards in the bins and at intervals thereafter, the red cards are checked and an inventory of the number of pieces of each item on hand is counted. An inventory printout of every red card item in stock is obtained.

THE NEXT STEP AFTER IDENTIFYING "NON-MOVERS"

Here are the procedures to follow to release investments in dead or non-moving items:

(a) Contact manufacturers directly by mail or through a local representative or regional manager, if one services your area, and request permission to return the non-moving item or items for credit.

(b) Contact the manufacturer and ask permission to exchange non-moving items in stock for other items in the line for which there is an active current demand.

(c) Ask the manufacturer to issue a credit memorandum for a non-moving item or items so that these items may then be rebilled on the same date on a 90, 120 or 180 day dating basis. With this procedure, the items remain on your shelves and while you have some nominal warehousing costs involved, you remove the investment in these items from your company to your supplier. (Inventory, *less accounts payable* is part of the net assets definition for purposes of making monthly cost of money charges). *Your* inventory investment is reduced.

Will the manufacturer do any of these things? The answer is, "yes." Ask and find out. The preference usually is to issue credit then rebill on a "dating basis." This procedure avoids costly handling and shipment expenses for both distributor and manufacturer as well as loss of time and wear and tear on the merchandise because of excessive handling.

(d) Remove item from stock in a close out or at a low price or discount if special pricing would move that type of item. This is a final alternative and sometimes a costly one, but not nearly as costly as having that item sit on your shelf month after month. Get your cost out of the item if you can and put that money in merchandise that is moving.

(e) One final consideration; if a favorable response is obtained to a request for "dating," you may want to consider passing on all or a portion of that "dating" as a special to your customers to get early consumer exposure of the item at retail and thus insure or at least give advantage to the possibility of display, sell-through and payment by your customer when dating terms have expired.

Persistent follow up is essential when non-movement identifications have been made.

RESULTS

One pharmaceutical distributor, rapidly expanding the number of pharmaceutical distribution centers in operation, reduced overall inventory investments by some eighteen million dollars in 90 days without adversely affecting service levels.

One of the primary techniques used to accomplish this was simply to identify and eliminate all non-moving items. The Red Card System was used and found to be effective. A simple, visual, manual procedure worked. It will work for you.

There has been a tendencey in the past for management to generalize and issue meaningless bulletins concerning inventory reductions. For instance, in this case, a total inventory reduction objective of eighteen million dollars could have been approached by parcelling out the inventory reduction required for each division, based on overstock calculations, and following up this assignment with urgent bulletins saying, "Come on fellows, let's get the job done . . . . etc." Bulletins of this kind should be put in the paper shredder and not mailed. You would at least save the postage and the reading time. Specific tactics are needed to identify and get rid of those items you are not selling. The general approach usually results in following the easiest procedure and that is to reduce purchase quantities on the faster moving items. This gets *quick inventory reduction results* and *high omission rates.*

It appears to be a strange paradox, but excessive inventory investments usually breed excessive omission rates—the higher the inventory investment, the greater the number of shorts or omissions. At the risk of redundancy, I have reiterated a point here, but Management must realize that heavy inventories do not insure a low omission rate. Buyers must understand this fact and know that Management has a high degree of sensitivity to it.

Identifying the non-moving items not only reduces inventory investment but is an aid to correct buying procedures as well. Something good happens when you walk through a warehouse and you see all of those red card facings. Pull a billing card from each bin. Make an item count and print out a list of non-movers and watch as your company inventory investment moves into those items that are selling.

You say, "we know the items that are not moving" — but, do you?

The Red Card System is a visual constant reminder of where your dead inventory dollars are invested.

Care should be taken to be sure the buyers properly note their stock cards that the red card items were eliminated from stock in some way other than normal sales. Stock cards must be marked "item discontinued" and no reorders placed.

In a computer buying system, the computer has to be notified that the red card item movement from stock was not a sale and not to reorder. Computer records must reflect all red card items as discontinued items, not to be reordered until such time as your normal movement and inventory levels indicate that buying should be resumed.

The *Red Card System*—try it, it works!

6

DECREASING WAREHOUSE AND DELIVERY COSTS THROUGH CUSTOMER EVALUATION FOR OPERATIONS AND SERVICE PLANNING: INCREASING SALES UP TO 50% AND MORE

If your order filling line is often loaded with too many small orders (shorts placed by customers who trade primarily with one of your competitors) and if each truck run has too many stops, your service to primary customers is adversely affected. Here is a procedure that can provide selectivity and remedy your service problem both in the warehouse and on delivery routes while effecting worthwhile economies. Evaluate your customers, providing primary service to primary accounts.

THE CHALLENGE

The survey of accounts by volume category is nothing new for the Sales Department. It is something new for operations use in setting up order-filling sequences and scheduling delivery routes.

An excessive number of orders (large and small) are scheduled for processing. There are too many store stops or deliveries on each delivery route to provide reliable good service to primary customers.

The order filling line has a limited number of lineal feet and will accommodate just so many order filling boxes. Our object is to give primary service to our primary customers and not clutter up the order filling line with small orders from customers buying primarily from competitive sources and using us for "shorts" or fill-ins to supplement a poor buying job and high omission rate of a competitor.

In addition to the order line congestion, it takes just as much time for the driver of a delivery truck to park and deliver a small, low-line extension order in a paper sack as it does to deliver a large general order. Stops average about 15 minutes each—finding a parking place, locating the invoice, extracting the invoice, delivering the merchandise and getting a signature on the delivery slip. This time factor is a variable in different markets depending upon distances, population density, freeway access and parking problems. So, if you have ten little short orders to deliver on a run, you delay service to primary customers up to two hours and a half on each scheduled truck run. The arithmetic looks like this:

> 10 non-profit, accommodation stops at 15 minutes per stop, counting driving time, and we have 150 minutes or a cumulative delay of 2½ hours on the truck run.

With delivery trucks out at peak traffic hours in the morning or afternoon, the delay can be even greater. Thirty stops is the desirable maximum for each scheduled truck run.

Too many stops and slow delivery schedules increase overtime costs and result in poor service to primary customers. This is a costly combination that adversely affects sales, increases operating costs and decreases profits. This is what results from lack of selectivity in order processing. Is this what you want?

You can serve the needs of your customers equally if you insist, but it is costly. Bear in mind the fact that the needs of your customers are by no means the same.

SAMPLE PROBLEM

When a retailer receives his daily order from a competitor in the morning, he checks his invoice for "shorts" and immediately calls these items into your telephone sales department as a waiting order or insists on same day delivery. What do you get for this effort to serve that customer? In a word—nothing—nothing but trouble. The account refuses to see your salesman; he won't permit a stock check or access to his "want book." These stores often have close financial ties with another supplier.

This order and all other similar ones received should be put in a deferred processing box and released only when the order filling line is empty and the complete orders have been accumulated and scheduled for delivery together, as one stop. Then, only on those days when delivery schedules permit, without undue delay in handling, you could make on time deliveries for primary customers.

Talk to those accounts using you as a back-up supplier or source of "shorts" or "omissions." Explain to them why your company must accumulate small orders for delivery one day a week on a day and delivery schedule of your choice. Your "short" customer will understand the problems. He may not like it, but he will understand why he can't simply use you. Solicit his preference for your company as his primary supplier.

When you get back to the office write a friendly letter something like the one illustrated in Figure 6-1.

Mr. John Doe
Doe Drug Center
Anywhere, U.S.A.

Dear John:

It was pleasant meeting and visiting with you this morning in your store there in Anywhere.

Your store was neat, clean, orderly and the merchandise well displayed, reflecting interested, capable management. The store was quite active with a good customer flow during our visit. I congratulate you upon your operations which are obviously successful.

We reviewed the economics involved which makes it impossible for this company to continue to provide preferential or primary daily delivery service on small fill-in orders. In addition to an out-of-pocket loss, we delay deliveries to primary customers who favor this company with the bulk of their purchases because our prices are competitive and our delivery service and omission rates are superior to competitive sources of supply. We work hard at maintaining reliable on time delivery schedules and this can only be done through the use of a system of order scheduling. You run a profitable operation and as a good businessman you understand and appreciate the cost factors involved.

We would welcome the opportunity to service you as a primary supplier and look forward to servicing your needs in an increasing way in the future as your business continues to grow, which we have every confidence that it will. We have reviewed our problem in a friendly, forthright manner, but it is really not so much our problem as it is a mutual one.

Thank you for the time devoted to our visit this morning during a busy day and thank you for your understanding and appreciation of the mutual problem discussed. I hope to see you again soon. We would like to have you as a primary customer and welcome your patronage on that basis.

You and your associates have our best wishes.

Sincerely,

Richard Rowe, Manager
Division "A" Company

Figure 6-1

Keep your visit pleasant. Avoid abrasiveness and never fail to take advantage of an opportunity to write a business letter under pleasant circumstances. Follow this up with brief subsequent visits as time and opportunity permit, and the account potential warrants. The Division Manager, Financial Services Manager, Operations Manager and Sales Manager can and should all participate in these contacts to develop new business. Time the visits carefully, don't "swamp" your potential customer with oversolicitation. Remember, he is a busy man too. Caution! Brief your Operations Manager carefully. He should be a good listener and indicate a desire to service the account. There should be no pressing, no promising (except within established delivery time schedules), no discussion of other accounts serviced. He should make notes of customers' comments.

You have heard it before: "The Sales Department is not the whole company but the whole company is the Sales Department." But, do you know what it means and do you in truth and in fact employ this concept? You should, because it does pay off.

As new electronic order entry systems reduce people-customer contact and with frequency of salesman contacts declining, build a close liaison between the "doers" in your business and your customers. Keep it a people-to-people business on a sound and constructive basis in this way. The more responsible contacts a customer has in the house you operate, the more at home he feels. Help him to feel at home through personal contact, meaningful follow-up and a lot of positive thoughts about your company or division and its services. Once you get him, your services will keep him at home.

Customers are not interested in your problems; they have plenty of their own. Their interest is "What's in it for me?" In the sample letter we have sought to stress the mutual nature of the problem and to offer primary service for a primary account. That's "what's in it" for your customer—an invitation to qualify for primary service on all purchases. The arithmetic is clear and simple. He has a choice and you invite qualification for primary service.

Referring to the Division "A" Example Figure 6-2, we find that,

44% of the accounts serviced bought less than $1,000.00 per month and accounted for only 2.75% of total volume, and

Almost half of the order filling line and half of the delivery stops produced less than 3% of the volume.

Let's look at the other end of this survey. 2.57% of the accounts bought over $10,000.00 per month and accounted for 29.8% of total sales, and less than 3% of the accounts serviced produced almost 30% of total volume.

The Division could lose almost half of its accounts, the low end volume ones, and the sales loss would be less than 3% (2.75%).

So, it makes sense to provide primary service to primary accounts. If you lost all 177 of the low volume accounts (44% of total accounts) you would free up your operations to better service the accounts that prefer your division as a primary supplier and would more than make up the nominal loss in sales (2.75%) to the large number of low volume accounts by improved service and sales increases to primary accounts.

Are the low volume accounts small stores? No, as a general rule they are large operations with a preference for another wholesaler as a source of supply. No discrimination against the small store is involved.

Review other examples set out at the conclusion of this chapter. The pattern reflects an astonishing degree of uniformity. Numerous other schedules including a variety of companies could be given. They exist but are repetitious in nature and, hence, would add no new value to our information, only emphasis as to the need for customer evaluation for operations use.

The conversion of short order buyers to primary accounts is not the result of the Sales Department's efforts so much as it is the result of consistently improved and constantly maintained service levels such as:

1. early, accurate and expeditious order processing,
2. dependable delivery scheduling.

A pharmacy owner or manager is more concerned with a reliable, consistent delivery at about the same time each day than he is in early deliveries that may vary widely from day to day.

A broad fluctuation in the number of stops a delivery truck must make, taking care of a changing number of low end volume accounts (short orders), results in inconsistent delivery schedules.

Why does the retailer want to depend on "same time each day" deliveries? Here is one reason:

One of the pharmacy's good customers comes in and asks for an item that the retailer does not have. He tells the customer, "I am out of that item now, but it is on order and if you will drop by again after lunch, say at 2 P.M., I will have it for you." The proprietor of this store is depending on a noon delivery or earlier. If it does not materialize, he has a problem with his own customer, the consumer. A prescription item may be involved in which time of medication may be essential. So, reliability as to time of delivery is important.

Other factors may be such things as availability of personnel to receive, check and shelve the merchandise. The arrival of an order before the morning shift leaves, in some stores, results in a savings and is a help to the pharmacy owner/manager.

SALES RESULTS

Did I say "operations use only?" Look what happened to sales. Let's review some of the recent sales increases of the sample divisions discussed in this chapter.

CURRENT SALES INCREASES

Division A	55.7% +
Division B	28.8% +
Division C	23.4% +
Division D	48.7% +
Division E	32.9% +
Division F	52.8% +

CURRENT SALES INCREASES

Division G	37.7% +
Division H	23.6% +
Division I	9.8% +
Division J	49.1% +
Division K	21.9% +
Division L	24.8% +

And now for a look at operating expense comparisons:

Operating Costs as a Percent of Sales

	Prior Year	*Current Year*
Division A	7.8%	7.0%
Division B	11.7%	10.8%
Division C	9.1%	8.4%
Division D	9.0%	8.3%
Division E	9.1%	8.4%
Division F	9.6%	8.6%
Division G	11.0%	10.5%
Division H	9.1%	8.4%
Division I	10.0%	9.8%
Division J		
Division K	10.4%	9.5%
Division L	9.4%	8.0%

The current industry average operating costs exceed 11%.

Other factors have contributed to this favorable arithmetic. Reference is made to Chapters 1, 2, 3, 4, 6, 7, 8, 9 and 10, outlining new management techniques that have a cumulative impact on improved operating figures and increased profits. Chapter 5 is not mentioned as having a direct bearing on this arithmetic because the matter of sales and operating costs are involved in these numbers and not inventory investments or imbalance, except in a very remote way.

And now for a review of other *customer evaluation for operations and service planning* reports. The additional reports to which we have referred, set out by Division, are shown, each complete and with space for making notes and working out your own computation. You might want to survey your own divisions or set out your own figures, if you have a single house operation.

Delivery costs drop

In addition to improved service to primary customers, delivery costs dropped from 1.3% to 1.1%, while labor contract rates were increasing substantially.

How long has it been since your delivery costs have declined as a percent of sales?

Let's review Customer Evaluation Schedules "B", "C", "D", "E", "F", "G", "H", "I", "J", "K", and "L"—Figures 6-3 through 6-13. Relate this information to the *operating cost schedules* given and to the *sales increase schedules* previously listed in this chapter. Get out a pencil and a pad. You will find, that the largest sales increases and the better improvements in operating costs as a percent of sales are generally found in those operations with the broadest opportunities to eliminate low volume accounts and concentrate improved service to primary accounts for increased volume. Any account can become a primary account and qualify for primary service schedules.

Management's problem is simply to get the most productive use of the facilities available. This will be a continuing challenge—to make better accounts out of "low end" or marginal volume customers. Again, this has little or nothing to do with the size of the store or its sales volume. It has everything to do with where any store is inclined to place its patronage and the reasons for that inclination. Meaningful leads for this may be found in Part III of this volume.

Our examples in this chapter have been in the drug distribution field because this is a high volume, service oriented business at all levels—direct shipping manufacturer, distributor and retailer. It is a very volatile high volume, high investment consumer business that is the day-to-day essence of the market place. New items, changing product mix and effective results of advertising and product promotion are important factors. These are felt immediately and contribute to market sensitivity.

Other, less sensitive examples could be cited in other industries but the results would bear out the same facts with similar conclusions. The profile would simply be more on the flat side and therefore less quickly perceived.

A wide geographic area is covered in the examples and the divisions set out in the schedules may not necessarily be divisions of the same company. In fact, they are not. Our object was and is to report representative results of the use of a new concept in account analysis—sales sources related to service levels, operating costs, and, arriving indirectly back at the alpha of all sales analysis information, how to use that information to improve sales. Have you used an account volume analysis in working with operations? It is the best way to:

- increase sales
- reduce operating costs
- improve operating profits.

In summary, *Customer evaluation for operations and service planning:*

1. makes for a smooth, economical operations flow
2. improves customer service
3. reduces operating costs
4. reduces delivery costs
5. increases sales
6. increases profits.

Figure 6-2

Customer Evaluation Schedule
Division A

No. of Accounts	% to Total	From	To	Total Purchases 2 Months	Monthly Average	% to Total Per Month
177	44.0	000	999	$ 62,367	$ 31,208	2.75
53	13.1	1,000	1,999	154,963	77,470	6.82
39	9.7	2,000	2,999	189,905	94,943	8.36
38	9.4	3,000	3,999	266,490	133,247	11.74
21	5.2	4,000	4,999	185,538	92,765	8.17
12	2.9	5,000	5,999	132,036	66,015	5.81
16	3.9	6,000	6,999	208,624	104,309	9.19
12	2.9	7,000	7,999	180,704	90,348	7.96
10	2.4	8,000	8,999	169,900	84,948	7.48
3	0.7	9,000	9,999	58,336	29,167	2.57
21	5.2	10,000 and Over		659,821	329,905	29.08
402				$2,268,684	$1,134,325	

Figure 6-3

Customer Evaluation Schedule
Division B

No. of Accounts	% to Total	From	To	Total Purchases 4 Months	Monthly Average	% to Total Per Month
212	41.4	000	999	$ 339,099	$ 84,653	7.66
127	24.8	1,000	1,999	719,258	179,732	16.27
71	13.8	2,000	2,999	695,145	173,509	15.71
24	4.6	3,000	3,999	333,536	83,374	7.54
18	3.5	4,000	4,999	332,050	83,005	7.51
15	2.9	5,000	5,999	330,737	82,677	7.75
10	1.9	6,000	6,999	262,793	65,695	5.94
7	1.3	7,000	7,999	209,022	52,254	4.73
3	0.5	8,000	8,999	98,993	24,748	2.24
7	1.3	9,000	9,999	264,062	66,012	5.97
18	3.5	10,000 and Over		834,383	208,638	18.89
512				$4,419,078	$1,104,297	

Figure 6-4

Customer Evaluation Schedule
Division C

No. of Accounts	% to Total	From	To	Total Purchases 2 Months	Monthly Average	% to Total Per Month
173	55.4	000	999	$ 75,786	$ 37,843	4.87
39	12.5	1,000	1,999	112,303	56,134	7.22
26	8.3	2,000	2,999	126,020	63,004	8.10
15	4.8	3,000	3,999	104,178	52,085	6.70
9	2.8	4,000	4,999	79,719	39,856	5.12
13	4.1	5,000	5,999	143,330	71,662	9.22
6	1.9	6,000	6,999	79,174	39,594	5.09
6	1.9	7,000	7,999	91,257	45,626	5.87
2	0.6	8,000	8,999	34,781	17,390	2.23
5	1.6	9,000	9,999	94,211	47,104	6.06
18	5.7	10,000 and Over		613,516	306,753	39.47
312				$1,554,275	$777,051	

Figure 6-5

Customer Evaluation Schedule
Division D

No. of Accounts	% to Total	From	To	Total Purchases 2 Months	Monthly Average	% to Total Per Month
281	59.0	000	999	$ 121,210	$ 60,590	7.03
80	16.8	1,000	1,999	215,489	107,724	12.50
27	5.6	2,000	2,999	127,972	63,980	7.42
20	4.2	3,000	3,999	142,458	71,225	8.27
17	3.5	4,000	4,999	147,277	73,634	8.55
10	2.1	5,000	5,999	108,169	54,082	6.27
14	2.9	6,000	6,999	179,514	89,754	10.42
5	1.0	7,000	7,999	74,279	37,139	4.31
3	0.6	8,000	8,999	50,671	25,335	2.94
2	0.4	9,000	9,999	37,449	18,724	2.17
17	3.5	10,000 and Over		518,063	259,009	30.07
476				$1,722,551	$861,196	

Figure 6-6

Customer Evaluation Schedule
Division E

No. of Accounts	% to Total	From	To	Total Purchases 2 Months	Monthly Average	% to Total Per Month
346	68.5	000	999	$ 115,676	$ 57,827	7.07
38	7.5	1,000	1,999	108,816	54,390	6.65
32	6.3	2,000	2,999	158,139	79,061	9.57
18	3.5	3,000	3,999	125,534	62,762	
15	2.9	4,000	4,999	136,260	68,126	
19	3.7	5,000	5,999	206,873	103,432	12.65
9	1.7	6,000	6,999	113,309	56,652	6.93
3	0.5	7,000	7,999	43,641	21,819	2.66
5	0.9	8,000	8,999	84,656	42,327	5.16
1	0.1	9,000	9,999	19,409	9,704	1.18
19	3.7	10,000 and Over		522,271	261,133	31.95
505				$1,634,584	$817,233	

Figure 6-7

Customer Evaluation Schedule
Division F

No. of Accounts	% to Total	From	To	Total Purchases 2 Months	Monthly Average	% to Total Per Month
240	59.8	000	999	$ 81,519	$ 40,735	4.58
43	10.7	1,000	1,999	129,160	64,572	7.27
26	6.4	2,000	2,999	127,919	63,947	7.19
16	3.9	3,000	3,999	118,269	59,130	6.65
10	2.4	4,000	4,999	87,741	43,869	4.93
18	4.4	5,000	5,999	201,873	100,934	11.36
12	2.9	6,000	6,999	157,116	78,555	8.84
8	1.9	7,000	7,999	119,442	59,719	6.72
8	1.9	8,000	8,999	133,210	66,603	7.49
0		9,000	9,999	0	0	
20	4.9	10,000 and Over		620,261	310,125	34.91
401				$1,776,510	$888,189	

Figure 6-8

Customer Evaluation Schedule
Division G

No. of Accounts	% to Total	From	To	Total Purchases 2 Months	Monthly Average	% to Total Per Month
106	41.7	000	999	$ 72,310	$ 36,133	5.06
42	16.5	1,000	1,999	114,659	57,319	8.02
21	8.2	2,000	2,999	102,241	51,117	7.16
21	8.2	3,000	3,999	147,683	73,867	10.34
19	7.4	4,000	4,999	167,308	83,650	11.71
12	4.7	5,000	5,999	132,472	66,234	9.27
6	2.3	6,000	6,999	78,248	39,122	5.48
7	2.7	7,000	7,999	104,259	52,127	7.30
3	1.1	8,000	8,999	52,446	26,223	3.67
3	1.1	9,000	9,999	58,120	29,059	4.07
14	5.5	10,000 and Over		397,996	198,996	27.87
254				$1,427,742	$713,847	

Figure 6-9

Customer Evaluation Schedule
Division H

No. of Accounts	% to Total	From	To	Total Purchases 2 Months	Monthly Average	% to Total Per Month
84	43.9	000	999	$ 36,680	$ 18,329	3.66
26	13.6	1,000	1,999	75,172	37,581	7.51
18	9.4	2,000	2,999	92,503	46,247	9.24
20	10.4	3,000	3,999	140,795	70,391	14.07
8	4.1	4,000	4,999	71,342	35,669	7.13
8	4.1	5,000	5,999	88,884	44,441	8.88
9	4.7	6,000	6,999	118,262	59,129	11.81
4	2.0	7,000	7,999	58,300	29,148	5.82
5	2.6	8,000	8,999	85,906	42,952	8.58
2	1.0	9,000	9,999	36,655	18,327	3.66
7	3.6	10,000 and Over		196,100	98,048	19.59
191				$1,000,599	$500,262	

Figure 6-10

Customer Evaluation Schedule
Division I

No. of Accounts	% to Total	From	To	Total Purchases 2 Months	Monthly Average	% to Total Per Month
116	58.5	000	999	$ 43,282	$ 21,618	4.91
22	11.1	1,000	1,999	61,853	30,921	7.03
21	10.6	2,000	2,999	107,814	53,902	12.25
3	1.5	3,000	3,999	21,578	10,788	2.45
5	2.5	4,000	4,999	45,859	22,928	5.21
6	3.0	5,000	5,999	65,866	32,931	7.48
4	2.0	6,000	6,999	51,332	25,665	5.83
4	2.0	7,000	7,999	60,868	30,433	6.91
5	2.5	8,000	8,999	85,615	42,806	9.73
4	2.0	9,000	9,999	76,402	38,200	8.68
8	4.0	10,000 and Over		259,294	129,646	29.47
198				$879,763	$439,838	

Figure 6-11

Customer Evaluation Schedule
Division J

No. of Accounts	% to Total	From	To	Total Purchases 2 Months	Monthly Average	% to Total Per Month
102	33.2	000	999	$ 60,180	$ 30,103	2.75
74	24.1	1,000	1,999	208,784	104,374	9.54
23	7.4	2,000	2,999	114,167	57,080	5.22
20	6.5	3,000	3,999	137,750	68,869	6.29
16	5.2	4,000	4,999	143,319	71,654	6.55
16	5.2	5,000	5,999	175,473	87,732	8.02
5	1.6	6,000	6,999	63,816	31,906	2.91
3	2.6	7,000	7,999	119,448	59,722	5.46
4	1.3	8,000	8,999	67,556	33,777	3.08
7	2.2	9,000	9,999	132,254	66,125	6.04
32	10.4	10,000 and Over		964,147	432,063	44.08
397				$2,186,894	$1,093,405	

Figure 6-12

Customer Evaluation Schedule

Division K

No. of Accounts	% to Total	From	To	Total Purchases 2 Months	Monthly Average	% to Total Per Month
97	34.1	000	999	$ 52,596	$ 26,234	2.77
36	12.6	1,000	1,999	102,112	51,052	5.40
31	10.9	2,000	2,999	153,434	76,706	8.11
24	8.4	3,000	3,999	166,763	83,374	8.82
21	7.3	4,000	4,999	190,171	95,083	10.06
19	6.6	5,000	5,999	207,207	103,599	10.96
13	4.5	6,000	6,999	167,567	83,781	8.86
12	4.2	7,000	7,999	179,978	89,985	9.52
14	4.9	8,000	8,999	234,151	117,072	12.38
5	1.7	9,000	9,999	96,801	48,399	5.12
12	4.2	10,000 and Over		309,332	169,662	17.95
284				$1,890,015	$944,947	

Figure 6-13

Customer Evaluation Schedule

Division L

No. of Accounts	% to Total	From	To	Total Purchases 2 Months	Monthly Average	% to Total Per Month
219	65.3	000	999	$ 62,124	$ 30,987	5.61
32	9.5	1,000	1,999	96,365	48,174	8.73
16	4.7	2,000	2,999	76,312	38,150	6.91
22	6.5	3,000	3,999	154,399	77,195	13.99
9	2.6	4,000	4,999	81,241	40,632	7.36
9	2.6	5,000	5,999	97,240	48,618	8.81
6	1.7	6,000	6,999	78,741	39,369	7.13
7	2.0	7,000	7,999	106,602	53,300	9.66
4	1.1	8,000	8,999	69,278	34,639	6.27
2	0.5	9,000	9,999	38,104	19,051	3.45
9	2.6	10,000 and Over		243,008	121,502	22.02
335				$1,103,414	$551,617	

$\frac{251}{84}$ = Accts. under $2000 per Mo. = $79,161 per Mo. Val. or 14.34% of Val.

84 = $551,617 less $79,161 =
$472,456.

One final comment on the Operations area; if you have not made a recent study of existing delivery schedules, do it now. In the recent past, the better stores with high volume and growth potential may have been in the area nearest your operations. These stores may continue to receive early-stop deliveries although volume has eroded and a hospital center many miles distant or an outlying shopping center may be where the high volume and future growth potential are today. Take a look at all of your delivery schedules and run some sales figures against the accounts as listed. You quite likely will want to revise some truck runs to start at the outlying accounts and work back toward the warehouse. You may say, "this is my traffic manager's responsibility, or my operations man or my shipping clerk." O.K., agreed! But look at a few of your delivery route lists anyhow and see if the delivery sequence satisfies you.

7

GENERATING ADDITIONAL STREAMS OF PROFIT THROUGH NEW MERCHANDISING SERVICES TECHNIQUES: THE DESIGN AND MERCHANDISING DEPARTMENT

A New Management Technique That Results in Measurable Customer Improvement, Increasing Sales and Profits

THE CHALLENGE

The face of competition during the next ten years will be little different than it is today. The point is to first recognize and then to intelligently evaluate the effectiveness of your competition. Then do something positive and constructive to meet it. Be proactionary and not reactionary in this effort.

Who is your competition; a nearby operation in your line of business? No! Your competition is anyone who offers goods or services in an effort to attract the consumer dollar. An available consumer dollar spent, but not on your product, is lost to competition. That competition may be an automobile dealer, a beauty shop, the super market or a show, travel plans, insurance programs or anything else that dips into the available funds of the consumer, our source of sales and profits. Consumer funds are limited. Many either-or decisions must be and are, made because of this limitation.

Now that we have identified competition, let's take a look at the "face of the consumer," our target source of increased sales and profits. Here we find significant and far-reaching changes developing.

While the face of competition will remain relatively unchanged, some proactionary planning is required now to effectively handle changing consumer patterns. This chapter will open new doors for you in this area.

The consumer in America:

- is a woman, primarily buying goods or services for herself, her husband, if married, and for her family. Women spend 8 out of 10 "consumer dollars" and the figures have been in this range for a long time. Source of money - "family funds" or joint bank account with the husband who regularly deposits his salary check or earnings in the "joint account."

- is an alert, informed, intelligent shopper and in the past somewhat given to "impulse buying" of attractively displayed, value marked, new items. Men seldom look at or buy anything other than the item they entered the store to buy in the first place. Women are more curious about new products and/or new brands.

- A new dimension is present for women now, not heretofore a factor in their buying habits. As a result of "Women's Lib" many women are themselves in upper income brackets *where they should be*, and they will be spending their own money. That is, money, in substantial amounts, that they themselves have earned personally. What effect this will have on her past "impulse buying" habits remains to be seen. Will she be more conservative with her own money? Will she now tend to concentrate her purchases on "things that last"? Will she now tend to buy more luxury items with her new and substantial income source added to available "family funds" for spending on family needs? Whatever she does, she is your primary consumer market. She will have more money to spend, not less money in the future as some "doomsday" prophets suggest. Understand her, please her and you will win.

- She likes to shop in pleasant, colorful, attractive, well lighted surroundings with convenient parking arrangements.

- Goods that are not clearly price marked are not for sale to her

- She is curious and thus, informed. Count on her continued interest in "impulse items."

- She is more affluent and has far more financial freedom than all of the women shoppers that have preceded her.

To summarize: your customer is a woman, she has more money to spend, she is informed and curious about new items, she likes (in fact, demands) a pleasant shopping environment. Are you prepared to serve her? If not, get ready because she is a power in the consumer market and the revolution is just beginning. Attractive packaging, attractive displays, pleasant, colorful, clean, well lighted stores were never more important to successful merchandising than they are today and will be tomorrow and for decades to come.

This then is the premise:

* we know our competition and it is varied and formidable
* we know our primary market and it is intelligent, informed and has been handling the shopping assignment for a long time. Substantially more money is and will coninue to be available in the future for most shoppers, so buying capability is there. How does our marketing or selling capacity "stack up"?

Proactionary moves for you to consider now center around the fact that the facilities of most retail businesses are obviously in need of refurbishing. Many stores are old, dirty, poorly lighted and badly arranged for effective modern merchandising. Some of your customers are among them and they will need your help. This is particularly true of the owner-management store without any kind of a supervisor's check list other than the owner's eye and awareness. Deterioration is gradual and the owner who enters and leaves his store every day by the front door does not see the paint peeling from the front door nor the worn spot on the floor just inside that door. He is accustomed to what he sees and only vaguely thinks about getting around to improvements some day. His customers, particularly new ones, see these things and are repulsed by them. Their impression is negative at the front door. Many will never return. Others who do will soon drift away to cleaner, more modern places to shop. And they should. How can one be sure that stocks are fresh and inventories clean when the very "welcome mat" of the store indicates just the opposite impression.

What practical plans or programs can be formulated and put to work to improve the quality and merchandising effectiveness of the retailer? Will they work? What will they cost?

The answer is yes they will work and they will make money instead of adding to your costs of doing business.

Let's look at a highly successful case history before getting into the "what to do," "how to do" and "look out for this" aspects of establishing a Design and Merchandising Department.

Following World War II, the facilities of most retail businesses were obviously in need of refurbishing. For ten years, shortages of metal and other materials had restricted any improvement to a limited "patchwork" procedure involving the use of old fixtures. Furniture and fixtures, with no replacements in ten years or more, had long since been "charged off." So the need for new and remodeled stores was there and so were the tax incentives.

Now shopping centers were being developed for new stores. Neighborhoods had been changing too. Everyone seemed to be moving further out and wanted nearby shopping conveniences.

I established a Design and Merchandising Department for a large, successful, publicly owned company to meet this need. The new department was built around the exceptional talents of a young designer and color coordinator with a good knowledge of the fixture and equipment business and the capacity to accurately draw plans and prepare complete specifications, as well as make effective color presentations. This talent plus customer needs resulted in a million dollar a year business the first year, each dollar of which in turn generated three additional dollars in merchandise sales. These sales, except for the improved merchandising capacity at retail, would not have materialized for our customer or our company.

The function of the Design & Merchandising Department was a new management technique used to meet a need and to help sell-through to the consumer. A complete design and installation service from one source was a far cry from the old concept of fixture selling—so many feet of wall cases, so many floor cases, a bobtail fountain unit, stools, etc. from several sources with lighting, colors, floor covering, and even store layout and design being up to the customer who had ideas, some very good ones. But he was, by no means, qualified to design and install a store or even remodel one. Terms of sale on new or remodeled installations were 25% with contract or order, and the balance payable monthly over a period of from 24 to 36 months plus prevailing interest rates.

The timing for the use of the new technique was precisely right. There had been a long period of inactivity. There was a need and D & M filled that need. We soon expanded the D & M Department to serve all divisions and all markets. D & M sales soared as did merchandise sales to the improved, more effective retail outlets. Today the bulk of company sales and sales increases continue to come from these stores and trends indicate that this situation will continue to prevail for decades in the future.

National, regional and local trade publications were quick to recognize the significance of this new development and gave extensive publicity to it, publishing photographs of many new and remodeled store installations and editorally pointing out some unique or new feature incorporated in each store. Within the next ten years, every other store operating in the subject company's market was to become a D & M installation. Half of the entire market had been put in the "competitive ball game" with a "good big bat." During the 1950's and 60's, every third day of each year saw a new D & M installation started somewhere in the market. Today's opportunities are even greater for the reasons given earlier in this chapter.

Opening order programs were developed for new stores and stock replenishment order programs were developed for remodeled outlets.

Orders were written, filled, packed and invoiced by retail drug store designated departments for more efficient receiving, checking and putting up stock by departments in the new or remodeled facilities.

In a growing business with sales, inventories and receivables all tending to increase, effective management controls are essential. We soon found that many of our customers now handling a substantial volume of sales with limited equity capital did not have access to even the most elementary accounting information that would provide the basis for maintaining the proper supervision over the five basic management controls. Elementary to be sure, but do not assume that your customers are getting this information at frequent enough intervals, if at all, to use it effectively. To meet this need we designed a "Monthly Analysis of Operations," or "Planned Profit Program." The subject of the Planned Profit

Programs is covered in detail in Chapter 8. Samples of forms used as well as numerous working examples are also provided in the following chapter.

In establishing an operation such as the Design and Merchandising Department within your company, experience gives us a clearly defined list of "do's" and "don't's".

There are several phases involved in setting up an effective and profitable department.

Phase one has to do with obtaining the services of an experienced fixture man who has the capacity to draw plans, including mechanical ones such as electrical, plumbing, curtain wall and drop ceiling plans. His services can be arranged for on a "fee basis" predicated upon the sale of an installation and the gross profit involved, or on a salary basis, or on a combination salary and commission arrangement. These men may be found and are available. Creativeness is important and desirable.

Phase two — contact an established fixture fabricating concern with a reputation for reliability; one that would be interested in a long-term relationship involving a series of installations over a period of years. Any modifications or changes on the job during installation should not involve an excessive charge if any charge at all. Discuss this frankly and work out an agreement.

Prepare a price list for your own use. Add 33-1/3% to your cost for a 25% gross profit on sales.

Do not buy a fixture plant or an interest in one. This is a completely separate business. It involves metal workers, wood workers, electrical workers, glaziers and other trades. It is also a "feast or famine" type of business—too much business or not enough to sustain operating costs. Avoid this involvement.

Do not over-emphasize quality to the extent that you create the impression that your customer is getting the finest fixtures built, but rather, make it clear that your fixtures are servicable, fairly priced and appropriate for the needs of his store. To over-emphasize quality will lead to the expectation of hand-rubbed, flawless jewelry cases which are neither needed nor could be afforded in most merchandising stores. Do not establish a basis for complaints and criticisms of quality by your own representations.

Keep a careful log on installation commitments. *Do not* schedule installations too close together.

Do not ask your Sales Department to canvass each salesman's territory for prospects at the outset of your program. A large backlog of prospects, even if carefully qualified, tends to disturb, disrupt and weaken your effectiveness.

Do concentrate on a few prospects and installations at a time. Give them full time and attention. *Do a thorough job.*

Tell the truth and insist that every man connected with the Department do the same. Credibility is essential to long range success and satisfied customers. There may be areas of disagreement, but there should never be an area of misunderstanding of facts or representations made.

Records, forms and their methodical use are essential to this operation. *You have access to them in this chapter.*

Competition, selling only fixture installations with a one-time sales involved, tends to cause overpromise or overcommitment. Follow-through is often lacking.

Build carefully, slowly and selectively. Do not vary from terms requiring a down payment of 25% of the total Fixture Contract.

A properly drawn Fixture Contract or Purchase Order should be prepared as well as a Fixture Note form and a Completion Certificate.

The signed note and signed completion certificate should be obtained the day installation is completed. Any delinquencies or things yet to be done to complete the job may be noted on the Completion Certificate as exceptions and should be handled without delay. Again, examples of all necessary forms may be found in this chapter.

When the sale and installation are complete, here is your position:

You really have a 50¢ dollar invested (down payment of 25% plus gross profit of 25%) and an interest income source at prevailing rates over a period of 24 months on a dollar that actually represents 75¢ (sales price less gross profit or your cost figure).

The Design & Merchandising Department filled an existing need in 1950 and the program is continuing to expand in the 1980's. The need still exists and will continue.

Marketing and merchandising developments since 1950 tend to emphasize the present and growing need for expanded design and merchandising services today with continued future growth assured.

If the quality of your customers is deteriorating in the market place, you will want to carefully evaluate this program which already has a highly successful "track record" over a period of 25 years. *To some degree, a distributor is responsible for the quality and effectiveness of the customers he serves!* If customer effectiveness can be improved, a distributor's business is just once removed from that improvement.

RESULTS

The results again are a profitable department, generating a million dollars in sales the first year and constantly growing each year thereafter, plus a record of $3.00 in additional merchandise sales each year for every $1.00 in equipment sales made during the year. This is a sell-through which requires no inventory and little investment.

The arithmetic looks like this:

1. Net before taxes and after cost of money charges—10% low to 12% high each fiscal year (as a percentage of sales).

2. Return on investment before taxes and after cost of money charges now—35%; can and has ranged much higher depending on job delivery dates and fiscal year closing dates.

3. Increased merchandise sales resulting and improved division profits are in addition to these earnings and this is where the big dollars are.

This is a self-supporting service department consistently generating additional regular merchandise sales and improving customer quality and effectiveness. Fixtures may be sold or leased.

Here are the required forms:

1. Conditional Sales Contract, Figure 7-1, in triplicate
2. Completion Certificate, Figure 7-2, in duplicate

3. Promissory Note forms, Figures 7-3 and 7-3A
4. Audit Status Form, Figure 7-4
5. Job Folder Forms with "check list," Figure 7-5 and
6. Cost Record on Fixture Installation, Figure 7-6. This is a confidential company record reflecting cost prices, sales prices and percentage of profit on installation. To qualify for a commission, a gross profit of 25% is required.

While the design and merchandising services outlined in this chapter constitute a unique and new management technique in drug and sundries distribution, similar opportunities exist in other fields.

Primary suppliers who perform the function of a kind of "small business administration" for their customers, fill a need, improve the effectiveness of outlets served, and prosper.

A Design & Merchandising Department established to remodel old stores as well as to install new ones should have the capability of providing:

1. Flat plans
2. Perspective drawings
3. Mechanical plans such as electrical and plumbing
4. Curtain wall plans
5. Floor coverings
6. Wall paper selection
7. Furniture and fixtues excluding cash registers and
8. Merchandise layout plans.

In short, the availability at one place of all necessary services to remodel an old store or install a new one is a great help to your customer and is usually appreciated.

No inventories are carried in any of the service catagories listed.

Contacts with sources of supply are maintained and floor covering or wall paper application (which are leasehold improvements actually, and become a part of the building), are paid for directly by the customer or perhaps a landlord or developer, depending upon arrangements agreed upon. These items are not included in fixture contracts nor are plumbing fixtures, water heaters, heating and air conditioning units and similar items.

For the smaller company, unwilling or unable to risk the relatively small equity investment or incur the nominal expense of a D & M Department, there is an alternative.

Work out an arrangement with a reliable local fixture manufacturing plant or plants if both wood and steel fixtures are involved. Visit a number of their recent installations and examine them as carefully as possible. Talk to the store owners about each installation. Dig for "pro's" and "con's" regarding each one's experience with the installation and the fixture fabricating plant handling it. If, as a rule ,the owner likes his store and feels that he has been fairly treated, make a credit check on the fixture company or companies involved. Work out an arrangement whereby you will provide qualified prospects for new fixture installations for a fee of 5%. This will be an on going arrangement subject to satisfactory performance on the part of the fixture manufacturer. The factory will bill the customer direct

CONDITIONAL SALES CONTRACT

1. DELIVERY. SUBJECT COMPANY shall have the right to deliver all the goods at one time or in portions from time to time. SUBJECT COMPANY shall not be liable for any failure to deliver or install hereunder where such failure has been occasioned by fire, embargo, strike, differences with workmen, failure to secure materials from usual sources of supply or any circumstances beyond the control of SUBJECT COMPANY not herein—above enumerated which shall prevent SUBJECT COMPANY from making delivery or installation in the usual course of business. SUBJECT COMPANY is not, however, relieved from making shipment or the BUYER from accepting delivery at the agreed price when the causes interfering with delivery shall have been removed.

2. WARRANTY. The Articles sold by SUBJECT COMPANY to BUYER pursuant to this agreement are expressly warranted to be free from manufacturing defects both in material and workmanship; however, the exclusive remedy of BUYER is limited to SUBJECT COMPANY replacing or repairing defective articles which are brought to the attention of SUBJECT COMPANY within one year from the date of installation. THIS WARRANTY IS EXPRESSLY IN LIEU OF ANY OTHER EXPRESS OR IMPLIED WARRANTIES INCLUDING ANY IMPLIED WARRANTY OF MERCHANTABILITY OR FITNESS.

3. INSTALLATION. The cost of installation in this contract has been figured on a straight—time basis, if, at the request of the buyer, the seller is required to install on an overtime basis, (i.e., at night or on holidays or on Saturday or Sunday) the buyer will be charged the difference between straight—time and overtime as an extra in addition to the control price. In addition, the seller will not be responsible for the removal of any existing fixtures, crates, or cartons other than to an area so designated for that place of business.

☐ Cash upon receipt of invoice

☐ Buyer agrees to sign Promisory Note and Security Agreement before shipment.

4. BUYER

Name of Store: _____

Name of Owner: _____
(Corporation: YES _____   NO ___)

Street: _____

City _____ County _____ State _____

5. LEGAL DESCRIPTION OF PREMISES

Lot No.: _____ Block No. : _____

Other : _____

6. RECORD OWNER OF REAL ESTATE: _____

Address of Owner : _____

7 AMOUNT OF SALE   _____

Tax on Sale :   _____

Total Purchase Price .   _____

Down Payment with Contract :   _____

Sales Tax :   _____

Total Down Payment :   _____

Deferred Balance :   _____

Number of Months :   _____

_____   _____
Salesman's Signature   Customer's Signature

FORM NO. 215   REV. 473

Figure 7-1

102

ACCEPTANCE OF DELIVERY AND COMPLETION

I (We), the undersigned, hereby certify that all apparatus, fixtures and other equipment have been furnished by SUBJECT COMPANY as described in our Equipment Lease Schedule, and that delivery and/or installation has been fully completed in accord with the terms of said Equipment Lease, and that the same has been accepted as satisfactory within the terms of same.

_____
LESSEE'S SIGNATURE

_____
DATE

Any exceptions or omissions are to be listed below:

(If none, so state)

_____

_____

_____

_____

_____

Figure 7-2

PROMISSORY NOTE

$ _____   _____, 19_____

                                                       _____

        Without grace, for value received, the undersigned (hereinafter referred to as
maker. whether one or more) jointly and severally promise to pay to the order of
____SUBJECT COMPANY_____ at its office at _____,
_____, the sum of _____
_____ Dollars, plus interest at the rate of ____ per
cent per annum on the unpaid balance from the ____ day of _____, 19_____.

        This note shall be paid in ____ successive monthly installments of $_____
each and one final installment of $_____ plus interest each month as it accrues.
The first installment is due and payable on or before the ____ day of _____,
19___, and the remaining installments are due on or before the ____ day of each month
thereafter until the full amount hereof has been paid.

        In the event default is made in the payment of any installment on this note, as
the same becomes due and payable, or if holder deems itself insecure, then the legal
holder hereof shall have the option, without demand or notice to the maker, to declare
this note immediately due and payable, and may thereupon exercise its rights set out
in the Security Agreement executed the ____ day of _____, 19___.

        All past due principal and interest on this note shall bear interest from
maturity of such principal or interest at the rate of ten per cent per annum.

        In the event default is made in the payment of this note, in whatever manner
its maturity may be brought about, and it is placed in the hands of an attorney
for collection, or is collected through the Probate Court or the Bankruptcy Court,
the makers promise to pay, as attorneys' fees, to the holder hereof, a reasonable
additional amount of not less than twenty per cent of the principal and interest due
on same at the time it is placed in the hands of said attorney for collection.

        Each maker, surety and endorser of this note waives notice, protest, presentment
and demand for payment and consents to the extension from time to time of this note
or any part hereof.

        Payment of this note is secured by the collateral described in a Security
Agreement between maker and payee dated the ____day of _____, 19___.

Address of Maker   _____

_____   _____

_____   _____

                                        _____

Form 15N
Rev. 2/75

Figure 7-3

104

Form 15
Rev. 1173

PROMISSORY NOTE

$_____   _____19____

The undersigned for value received hereby promises to pay to the order of _____SUBJECT COMPANY_____

_____DOLLARS

At its office at_____,_____,_____.
                     CITY   COUNTY   STATE

due and payable on the_____day of each month in the respective installments given below; with exchange and collection charges; with interest at_____% per annum on unpaid balances from_____, payable monthly as it accures. All installments of principal and interest shall bear interest at 10% per annum from their dates of maturity. If placed with an attorney for collection, a reasonable attorney's fee shall be added to what may be unpaid of this note, and if suit is brought, included in any judgment that may be rendered hereon. Failure to pay any installment when due shall at the option of the holder, without notice, mature all unpaid principal in this and on any other notes then owing by the undersigned.

MONTH	19____		19____		19____		19____		19____	
JANUARY										
FEBRUARY										
MARCH										
APRIL										
MAY										
JUNE										
JULY										
AUGUST										
SEPTEMBER										
OCTOBER										
NOVEMBER										
DECEMBER										

The makers, endorsers and all guarantors of this note severally waive presentment for payment, demand, protest and notice of protest, non-payment or dishonor, and also waive any and all defenses on the ground of any extensions or partial payment which may be granted or accepted by the holder before or after the maturity of this note or any part thereof.

ADDRESS OF MAKER:

_____

_____   _____[SEAL]

_____   _____[SEAL]

J-V No._____   _____[SEAL]

Figure 7-3A

Form 199   AUDIT STATUS
                          ACCOUNTS AND NOTES RECEIVABLE   DATE_____

STORE NAME AND ADDRESS_____

OWNER_____ _____ CORP._____ PARTNERSHIP _____ INDIVIDUAL _____

ORIGINAL FINANCING: DATE _____ OPEN ACCOUNT $_____ NOTE $_____

COLLATERAL: FIXTURES _____ MERCHANDISE _____ OTHER_____

EXPLAIN COLLATERAL:

INSURANCE COVERAGE: AMOUNT $_____ LOSS PAYABLE TO SWD? YES_____ NO_____

OTHER COMMENTS:

NOTE CLASSIFICATION: _____
                          D&M, Mdse., Other

DATE	TOTAL DUE		PAST DUE		REMARKS
	ACCOUNTS	NOTES	ACCOUNTS	NOTES	
MAY					
JUNE					
JULY					
AUGUST					
SEPTEMBER					
OCTOBER					
NOVEMBER					
DECEMBER					
JANUARY					
FEBRUARY					
MARCH					
APRIL					
MAY					

Figure 7-4

106

STORE NAME_____

ADDRESS_____

CITY & STATE _____

PHONE NO._____

OWNER'S NAME _____

MGR'S NAME _____

BUILDER'S NAME_____

ADDRESS_____

CITY & STATE _____

PHONE NO._____

```
┌─────────────────────────────────────────┐
│ FINAL INSTALLATION DATE _____ │
│ REVISED DATE _____ │
└─────────────────────────────────────────┘
```

ARCHITECT'S NAME_____

ADDRESS_____

CITY & STATE _____

PHONE NO._____

ADDITIONAL INFORMATION: _____
_____
_____
_____

FIXTURE JOB CHECK LIST

☐ __ _____ REQUEST FOR SERVICE RECEIVED

☐ __ _____ CHECK WITH DIVISION MANAGEMENT (CREDIT)

☐ __ _____ CONTACT CUSTOMER

☐ __ _____ CALL ON CUSTOMER

☐ __ _____ OBTAIN BLDG. PLANS OR MEASUREMENTS

☐ __ _____ DEVELOP PRESENTATION PLAN

☐ __ _____ PRESENT PRESENTATION PLAN

☐ __ _____ REVISE PLAN

☐ __ _____ PRICE JOB

☐ __ _____ PRESENT FINAL PLAN & PRICE

☐ __ _____ SIGN CONDITIONAL SALES CONTRACT

☐ __ _____ SELECT WOOD FINISH

☐ __ _____ SELECT WOOD FIXTURE INTERIOR COLOR

☐ __ _____ SELECT WOOD FIXTURE STYLE

☐ __ _____ SELECT WOOD FIXTURE BASE COLOR

☐ __ _____ SELECT LAMINATE PLASTICS

☐ __ _____ SELECT WALL COVERINGS

☐ __ _____ SELECT CARPET

☐ __ _____ SELECT SPECIAL ITEMS

☐ __ _____ SELECT STEEL COLORS (BACKS, SHELVES & BASE)

☐ __ _____ CONTRACT APPROVAL BY DIVISION MANAGEMENT

☐ __ _____ WRITE SPECIFICATIONS

☐ __ _____ DRAW MECHANICAL PLANS

☐ __ _____ INSTALLATION DATE PROMISED _____

☐ __ _____ VERIFY INSTALLATION DATE WITH FACTORY

☐ __ _____ DISTRIBUTE PLANS & SPECIFICATIONS
    SIX FIXTURE PLANS TO WOOD FACTORY & TWO MECHANICAL
    TWO FIXTURE PLANS TO STEEL FACTORY & ONE MECHANICAL
    ONE SET OF PLANS TO DIVISION MANAGER
    ONE SET OF PLANS TO CUSTOMER (OR AS REQUESTED)

☐ __ _____ ORDER WOOD FIXTURES

☐ __ _____ ORDER STEEL FIXTURES

☐ __ _____ ORDER CARPET

☐ __ _____ ORDER FOUNTAIN EQUIPMENT

☐ __ _____ ORDER "BUY OUT" ITEMS _____

☐ __ _____ _____

☐ __ _____ _____

☐ __ _____ _____

☐ __ _____ _____

☐ __ _____ _____

☐ __ _____ ORDER MISC. SPECIAL ITEMS _____

☐ __ _____ _____

☐ __ _____ _____

☐ __ _____ _____

☐ __ _____ _____

☐ __ _____ _____

☐ __ _____ VERIFY BLDG. MEASUREMENTS

☐ __ _____ SCHEDULE CARPET INSTALLATION

☐ __ _____ SCHEDULE STEEL INSTALLATION

☐ __ _____ SCHEDULE WOOD INSTALLATION

☐ __ _____ SCHEDULE FOUNTAIN INSTALLATION

☐ __ _____ CHECK FINAL INSTALLATION

☐ __ _____ OBTAIN COMPLETION CERTIFICATE

(EXCEPTIONS)_____
_____
_____
_____
_____

☐ __ _____ PAY ALL INVOICES

☐ __ _____ CHARGE OUT JOB

☐ __ _____ COMPLETE FORM 150

Figure 7-5

COST RECORD ON FOUNTAIN AND FIXTURE INSTALLATION

Job No._____   _____Division

Approved_____   _____Salesman

CUSTOMER_____ Date Sold_____

ADDRESS_____Completed_____

1. Contract Price $_____

2. Less: Invoice Cost of Equipment (Same as 7.)   _____

3. Less: Freight and Erection (Same as 8.)   _____

4. Total (2 and 3) $_____

5. Gross Profit (1 less 4) $_____

6. Gross Profit % (5 divided by 1)   _____%

Itemize Invoice Cost of Equipment   **Itemize Freight and Erection**

_____ $_____   _____ $_____

_____ $_____   _____ $_____

_____ $_____   _____ $_____

_____ $_____   _____ $_____

_____ $_____   _____ $_____

     7. Total $_____   8. Total $_____

IF MORE SPACE IS NEEDED USE BACK SIDE

COMPUTATION FOR COMMISSION

9. Contract Price (Same as 1) $_____

10. Less Freight and Erection (Same as 8) $_____

11. Net Sales Price (9 minus 10) $_____

12. Invoice Cost of Equipment (Same as 7) $_____

13. Remainder (11 minus 12) $_____

14. Per Cent of Sales Price (13 divided by 11)   _____%

COMMISSION PAYMENT

MAKE 3 COPIES
2 copies Division Accountant   _____ ____ % _____

1 copy D & M Job File   _____ ____ % _____

          _____ ____ % _____

Figure 7-6

and either carry the paper or place it with a bank. You will know the terms of the note but have no investment or other responsibility connected with it.

The 5% will possibly cover your expenses of following up the job plus some nominal commission for the salesman in whose territory the installation was made if he reported the prospect in writing at least 30 days before the contract date and assisted in the sale. There will be no profit in this arrangement for you but your customer will have improved facilities. He will sell more merchandise and you will replenish it.

Caution — the fixture manufacturer is making one sale and he is out of the picture. Your company will be soliciting business every day. If the customer is dissatisfied in any way with his installation he can and may indicate his displeasure by withholding business from your company or penalizing your sales. Stay in touch and make certain that the fixture people leave no loose ends or any reason for customer dissatisfaction. A form is available to help you with this, the "Completion Certificate." If your fixture manufacture people understand that business stops with the first dissatisfied customer, you will have little or no trouble.

Settlement of your fee is to be made upon billing of the installation to the customer. Your check, the Completion Certificate and the fixture note should all bear the same date.

Merchandising or proper stock arrangement and effective merchandise display in the new or remodeled store is essential. Your salesman and the customer should get together and work out a merchandise layout plan, using a copy of the flat plans of the store to designate departments and merchandise locations. If you have a competent Retail Merchandising Manager, this would be his duty.

Advantages of this alternative to establishing a fully operative D & M Department are:

- You have no D & M Department personnel expense
- You avoid billing the job and carrying or placing the equipment note; no investment here; no contingent liability
- You are in a position to exert meaingful influence with the fixture manufacturer to see that you customer gets what he understood he would get and of course, wants. You are not the direct target of any complaint since you did not sell the fixtures yourself
- You have upgraded the merchandising effectiveness of a retail outlet prone to patronize your company.

There are disadvantages:

a. You must rely upon people not supervised or controlled by you, to please your customer
b. Problems as to installation dates arise when you rely entirely upon the fixture manufacturer's setting and keeping those dates firm
c. Your customer's fixture job may be one of many being processed in the mill and quite possibly a comparactively small job, and it can be delayed or sidetracked for larger, more lucrative jobs in process

d. Missing parts, omissions or corrections noted on the "Completion Certificate" may not receive the prompt attention that should be given to them

e. You derive no profit from the fixture sale, usually 25% of sale

f. You derive no interest income from the fixture note secured by a security agreement and usually bearing a relatively high rate of interest since banks and other financial institutions do not generally look with favor on trade fixtures as collateral for a loan. The reason is understandable. Default on the loan would place the bank or lending institution in possession of fixtures it can't use or readily sell, but you are in that business and would in all probability place the fixtures promptly and probably at a profit.

I cannot call to mind a single instance of a loss having been incurred on a fixture note with a good security agreement. These notes are always for an amount not in excess of 75% of the purchase price of the fixtures, after a down payment of 25%. The notes provide for payment in 24 to 36 equal monthly installments which includes principal due and interest to date each month.

Whether the fixture company keeps the paper, places it with a bank or some other financial institution, it is desirable for your Financial Services Manager to set up a "Monthly Analysis of Operations" program with the customer involved and assist the store owner in trading cash flow each month to insure cash availability for note payments. This is another customer development service covered in the following chapter.

Sample forms used are shown and the procedure outlined in detail. The working examples given are simply that, examples taken at random. They are by no means intended as examples of good management.

It should be recognized also that tracing cash flow rarely works out to the penny or even to the dollar when gross profit estimates are used. This program is simply to generally determine the amount of earnings at monthly intervals and to trace those earnings. The object is to preserve them in the form of cash for use in debt reduction or debt retirement programs.

PART III
CUSTOMER DEVELOPMENT

Three New Ways to Build More Productive, Viable, Profitable, Prompt Paying Customers

8

MONTHLY ANALYSIS OF OPERATIONS: A PLANNED PROFIT PROGRAM FOR CUSTOMERS

Your customer needs help in supervising the five basic management controls in his business. Here is a proven system that makes friends for your company; converts marginal accounts into strong, viable, prompt paying customers; and provides a basic and constructive role for your financial services manager.

THE CHALLENGE

Customers in the "owner/manager" store category, with improved merchandising facilities and increasing sales volume seldom have access to even the most elementary operating information that will enable them to exercise the proper supervision over basic management controls. They have no effective way of tracing earnings and cash flow from month to month.

Operating expenses sometimes get out of hand.

There is lack of supervision over inventory control because of lack of timely and reliable information.

There is lack of supervision over accounts receivable control in some cases for the same reason.

A store handling a good volume of sales reflecting increases from month to month becomes a credit problem. Continuing sales to the customer are jeopardized.

What is the remedy? How can we salvage a high volume account and a potentially prompt paying one?

Working through our Financial Services Manager, the account is visited and a "Monthly Analysis of Operations" or "Planned Profit Program" is set up. The arrangement is verified by a letter of agreement—Figure 8-1.

Figures 8-2 through 8-2C illustrate the use of the Planned Profit Program in Subject A store over a period of four months.

Example

(Subject Store "A")

Here is a working example of how the Planned Profit Program, a cash flow tracing procedure, as well as an aid to supervision over the five basic management controls:

1. Sales
2. Gross Profit
3. Expenses
4. Inventory, and
5. Accounts Receivable

enabled a young new ownership/manager to balance his operations and pay for a valuable property, a profitable retail pharmacy, entirely out of the after tax earnings of the store itself.

The prior owner was an older man who had a favorable lease which together with renewal options extended over a period of ten years. He wanted to retire from the business and agreed to sell his store to a young man in whom he had confidence, taking a long term note and security agreement. The seller wanted interest income and set the note to be liquidated over a period of five to ten years. Tax considerations were in the picture as well as the desire for interest income. The seller accepted the note for $80,000 secured by a valid security agreement covering the assets of the store.

The new owner took over the operations of the store in September and after three months of operation during the better seasonal months of the year, he had not been able to accumulate enough cash to make a payment of any kind of the purchase money note. Moreover, he was permitting some supplier accounts to become delinquent for lack of payment.

Blank Date

Mr. John Doe
SUBJECT "A" STORE
Anywhere, U.S.A.

Dear John:

The purpose of this letter is to set out in some detail, the matters discussed and agreed upon this morning during our visit.

After a careful review of available accounting records, it was agreed that your operation handles sufficient sales volume at an adequate gross profit with operating expenses for the most part, effectively controlled, resulting in a reasonably adequate monthly operating profit.

The store's inability to pay debt results from:

1. excessive and increasing inventory investment
2. excessive and increasing accounts receivable investment.

Since inventories are high in relation to sales volume and are continuing to increase and the number of days outstanding on accounts receivable is high and has been growing, it was agreed that we would work on these two problem areas, using the money released each month from these excessive investments plus earnings and non-cash items of expense money available, to apply on an orderly debt reduction program.

As a tool for helping you monitor these controls and accurately trace your cash flow each month, it was agreed that on or before the 5th day of each month, you would forward to this office a completed Planned Profit Program form which we would review, making appropriate adjustments, additions and notations thereon. We would return the form promptly to you each month with a constructive letter of analysis. A pad of these forms is being mailed to you under separate cover for your use.

Monthly earnings, before taxes, are in the $2,000 per month range. Inventory and accounts receivable investments are so high that they provide opportunities to release another $5,000 each month from your operations with the bulk of this figure coming from inventory reductions. This curtailment in inventory investment should not adversely affect sales. It is anticipated that $5,000 to $7,000 will be available each month for use in debt reduction. Since monies will be needed for your April 15th tax payment and a payment of $5,000 on your purchase money note must be made, it is anticipated that the difference between these total figures and the monies released from operations will amount to approximately $3,000 or $1,000 per month during the next three months. This amount, plus accrued interest to date, you agree to pay on or before the 15th of each month. This accomplishment will retire the delinquent portion of the debt owed to this company.

Figure 8-1

Letter of Agreement

It is understood that all payment up to and including any present or future indebtedness due this company is payable at our offices at ___[Blank City]___ , ___[Blank County]___ , ___[Blank State]___ .

We look forward to working with you in the future and if there is anything in this letter that is not in accord with your understanding of our agreement, please let me hear from you promptly and we will make whatever adjustments appear to be in order.

If there are no questions regarding the accuracy of this memorandum prepared from my notes, please date and sign one copy of the letter in the space provided and return it to this office in the prepared envelope enclosed. Retain the original letter for your files.

While you have problems, they are not beyond correction through the use of the prompt remedial action which we have agreed to implement.

Your cooperation is appreciated and we look forward to servicing your needs in an increasing way as your business continues to grow in the future as we have every confidence that it will.

You have our best wishes.

Sincerely,

By _____
Richard Roe, Financial
Services Manager

AGREED:

_____

[Signature of Customer]

Fig. 8-1 (continued)

Letter of Agreement

The new proprietor was discouraged and came into our Financial Services Manager's office with two things:

1. The store's December 31 (current year) balance sheet or statement of assets and liabilities (showing comparative prior year figures) and
2. A copy of the store's last income tax return showing a substantial tax installment to be due for payment on April 15.

The comparative balance sheet (current) reflected three significant problem sources (all subject to remedial action):

1. Inventory investment had increased substantially and disproportionately to sales
2. Accounts receivable total was up with a growing percentage of delinquent accounts
3. The store had no cash to speak of (less than $500).

THE PLANNED PROFIT PROGRAM

(AN ANALYSIS OF MONTHLY BUSINESS)

SUBJECT "A" STORE	Anywhere, U.S.A.	January
Name of Store	Location	Month Year

	AMOUNT		
Charge Sales	$	6,325	07
Cash Sales		18,975	21

		AMOUNT		Your %	Av. %
Net Sales for Month	TOTAL $	25,300	28	100.0	100.0
Cost of Sales (Est.)		16,870	19	66.7	63.8
Gross Profit (Est.)		8,430	09	33.3	36.2

EXPENSES	AMOUNT		Your %	Av. %
Proprietor's Withdrawals $	1,000	00	4.0	7.8
Employees' Salaries	2,987	59	11.8	12.4
Rent	700	00	2.8	2.5
Heat)	117	19	.5	
Light & Power)	220	04	.9	0.7
Taxes & Licenses	450	49	1.8	1.6
Insurance	86	12	.3	0.9
Interest	466	67	1.8	0.4
Repairs	130	00	.5	0.4
Delivery		-0-	.0	0.3
Advertising	649	63	2.6	1.3
Miscellaneous	201	79	.8	2.8
Depreciation	274	00	1.1	0.9
Bad Debts Charged Off		-0-	.0	0.1
Telephone	93	55	.3	0.3

JANUARY CASH FLOW

Depreciation	$ 274.00
Operating Profit Before Taxes	1,779.06
Known Cash Flow	$2,053.06
INVENTORY REDUCTION	Unknown
ACCTS. RECEIVABLE REDUCTION	Unknown

THIS IS INITIAL REPORT

		AMOUNT		Your %	Av. %
Operating Expenses for Month	TOTAL $	7,377	07	29.2	32.4
Operating Profit or Loss		1,053	02	4.1	3.8
Other Income (Discounts, etc.)		726	04	2.9	
Net Profit or Loss for Month		1,779	06	7.0	

Total Purchases	$	16,520	09
Accounts Payable, Total		18,243	23
Notes Payable, Total		80,000	00
Accounts Receivable, Total		9,175	12
Bank Balance		379	62

INSTRUCTIONS: Fill in only AMOUNT of Sales for Month, AMOUNT of each item of expense applicable in your operations, other income, and your total purchases for month, listing accounts payable, receivable, and bank balance and notes payable as of the end of the month. The form will be completed and returned to you promptly with a memorandum setting out any constructive comments that appear in order.

Form 4

ANOTHER CUSTOMER SERVICE FURNISHED WITHOUT CHARGE BY

Figure 8-2

THE PLANNED PROFIT PROGRAM

(AN ANALYSIS OF MONTHLY BUSINESS)

SUBJECT "A" STORE	Anywhere, U.S.A.	February
Name of Store	Location	Month Year

Charge Sales	$	6,061 12
Cash Sales		18,190 10

	AMOUNT	Your %	Av. %
Net Sales for Month TOTAL $	24,251 22	100.0	100.0
Cost of Sales (Est.)	16,170 82	66.7	63.8
Gross Profit (Est.)	8,080 40	33.3	36.2

EXPENSES	AMOUNT	Your %	Av. %
Proprietor's Withdrawals $	1,000 00	4.1	7.8
Employees' Salaries	2,895 09	11.9	12.4
Rent	700 00	2.9	2.5
Heat	112 08	.5	
Light & Power	151 58	.6	.7
Taxes & Licenses	382 48	1.6	1.6
Insurance	86 12	.4	0.9
Interest	466 67	1.9	0.4
Repairs	25 40	.1	0.4
Delivery	-0-	.0	0.3
Advertising	500 00	2.1	1.3
Miscellaneous	142 65	.6	2.8
Depreciation	266 00	1.1	0.9
Bad Debts Charged Off	-0-	.0	0.1
Telephone	77 34	.3	0.3

FEBRUARY CASH FLOW

Depreciation		$ 266.
Operating Profit Before Taxes		1,958.
Cost of Sales	$16170.82	
Purch.	12091.10	

INVENTORY REDUCTION	$4,079.
ACCTS. RECEIVABLE REDUCTION	1,065.
Total Cash Flow	$7,369.

DISPOSITION

Accounts Payable Reduction	$3,000.00
Increase Bank Balance	4,369.74
Total Disposition	$7,369.74

	AMOUNT	Your %	Av. %
Operating Expenses for Month TOTAL $	6,805 41	28.1	32.4
Operating Profit or Loss	1,274 99	5.2	3.8
Other Income (Discounts, etc.)	684 00	2.8	
Net Profit or Loss for Month	1,958 99	8.0	

Total Purchases	$	12,091 10
Accounts Payable, Total		15,243 52
Notes Payable, Total		80,000 00
Accounts Receivable, Total		8,110 09
Bank Balance		4,749 36

INSTRUCTIONS: Fill in only AMOUNT of Sales for Month, AMOUNT of each item of expense applicable in your operations, other income, and your total purchases for month, listing accounts payable, receivable, and bank balance and notes payable as of the end of the month. The form will be completed and returned to you promptly with a memorandum setting out any constructive comments that appear in order.

Form 4   ANOTHER CUSTOMER SERVICE FURNISHED WITHOUT CHARGE BY

Figure 8-2A

THE PLANNED PROFIT PROGRAM

(AN ANALYSIS OF MONTHLY BUSINESS)

SUBJECT "A" STORE	Anywhere, U.S.A.	March	
Name of Store	Location	Month	Year

Charge Sales	$	7,012	12
Cash Sales		20,055	14

		AMOUNT		Your %	Av. %
Net Sales for Month	TOTAL $	27,067	26	100.0	100.0
Cost of Sales (Est.)		18,044	63	66.7	63.8
Gross Profit (Est.)		9,022	63	33.3	36.2

EXPENSES	AMOUNT		Your %	Av. %
Proprietor's Withdrawals $	1,000	00	3.7	7.8
Employees' Salaries	3,378	44	12.5	12.4
Rent	700	00	2.6	2.5
Heat	120	12	.4	
Light & Power	180	06	.7	.7
Taxes & Licenses	700	69	2.6	1.6
Insurance	86	12	.3	0.9
Interest	466	67	1.7	0.4
Repairs	20	13	.1	0.4
Delivery		-0-	.0	0.3
Advertising		-0-	.0	1.3
Miscellaneous	157	99	.6	2.8
Depreciation	266	00	1.0	0.9
Bad Debts Charged Off		-0-	.0	0.1
Telephone	77	35	.2	0.3

MARCH CASH FLOW

Depreciation	$ 266.
Operating Profit Before Taxes	2,589.
	$2,855.
Cost of Sales	$18044.63
Purch.	14041.10
INVENTORY REDUCTION	$4,003.
Total Cash Flow	$6,858.

DISPOSITION

Accounts Payable Reduction	$5,000.00
Accts. Receivable Increase	1,158.79
Bank Balance Increase	700.00
Total Disposition	$6,858.79

		AMOUNT		Your %	Av. %
Operating Expenses for Month	TOTAL $	7,153	57	26.4	32.4
Operating Profit or Loss		1,869	06	6.9	3.8
Other Income (Discounts, etc.)		720	20	2.6	
Net Profit or Loss for Month		2,589	26	9.5	

Total Purchases	$	14,041	10
Accounts Payable, Total		10,243	52
Notes Payable, Total		80,000	00
Accounts Receivable, Total		8,268	88
Bank Balance		5,449	36

INSTRUCTIONS: Fill in only AMOUNT of Sales for Month, AMOUNT of each item of expense applicable in your operations, other income, and your total purchases for month, listing accounts payable, receivable. and bank balance and notes payable as of the end of the month. The form will be completed and returned to you promptly with a memorandum setting out any constructive comments that appear in order.

Form 4   ANOTHER CUSTOMER SERVICE FURNISHED WITHOUT CHARGE BY

Figure 8-2B

THE PLANNED PROFIT PROGRAM

(AN ANALYSIS OF MONTHLY BUSINESS)

SUBJECT "A" STORE	Anywhere, U.S.A.	April	
Name of Store	Location	Month	Year

Charge Sales	$	6,671	10
Cash Sales		20,113	29

		AMOUNT		Your %	Av. %
Net Sales for Month	TOTAL $	26,784	39	100.0	
Cost of Sales (Est.)		17,856	26	66.7	
Gross Profit (Est.)		8,928	13	33.3	

EXPENSES	AMOUNT		Your %	Av. %
Proprietor's Withdrawals $	1,000	00	3.7	7.8
Employees' Salaries	3,370	35	12.6	12.4
Rent	700	00	2.6	2.5
Heat	102	84	.4	
Light & Power	240	18	.9	.7
Taxes & Licenses	391	59	1.5	1.6
Insurance	130	24	.5	0.9
Interest	466	67	1.7	0.4
Repairs	181	85	.7	0.4
Delivery	-0-		.0	0.3
Advertising	264	24	1.0	1.3
Miscellaneous	152	07	.6	2.8
Depreciation	266	00	.9	0.9
Bad Debts Charged Off	-0-		.0	0.1
Telephone	81	01	.3	0.3

APRIL CASH FLOW

Depreciation	$ 266.
Operating Profit Before Taxes	2,093.
	$2,359.
Cost of Sales	$17856.26
Purch.	15472.18
INVENTORY REDUCTION	$2,384.
Total Cash Flow	$4,743.

DISPOSITION

Accounts Payable Reduction	$130.29
Note Reduction	3,000.00
Accts. Receivable Increase	611.88
Bank Balance Increase	1,001.00
Total Disposition	$4,743.17

		AMOUNT		Your %	Av. %
Operating Expenses for Month	TOTAL $	7,347	04	27.4	32.4
Operating Profit or Loss		1,581	09	5.9	3.8
Other Income (Discounts, etc.)		512	00	1.9	
Net Profit or Loss for Month		2,093	09	7.8	

Total Purchases	$	15,472	18
Accounts Payable, Total		10,113	23
Notes Payable, Total		75,000	00
Accounts Receivable, Total		8,880	76
Bank Balance		6,449	36

INSTRUCTIONS: Fill in only AMOUNT of Sales for Month, AMOUNT of each item of expense applicable in your operations, other income, and your total purchases for month, listing accounts payable, receivable, and bank balance and notes payable as of the end of the month. The form will be completed and returned to you promptly with a memorandum setting out any constructive comments that appear in order.

ANOTHER CUSTOMER SERVICE FURNISHED WITHOUT CHARGE BY

Figure 8-2C

The young proprietor's attitude was: "Here I have worked long hours, I've increased the business, I have earned a profit in the store. I know that I have and yet, all I have to show for my effort is debt and past due accounts."

This young man's problem is not unique. Many proprietors can generate sales volume, maintain a satisfactory gross profit, control operating expenses and generate favorable earnings.

The problem lies in preserving these earnings in the form of cash. To do this, proper supervision must be maintained over inventory control and accounts receivable control.

Arrangements were made with the new store owner to fill out a Planned Profit Program form each month starting with the month of January and continuing for as long as any portion of the purchase price remained unpaid and beyond that time if the store owner wished to continue the service. Copies of each monthly cash flow report were to be mailed, at the new owner's request, to the noteholder.

Reference is made to the first report (January). The store's actual gross profit during the prior year based on physical inventory counts was 35%. A decision was made to use a conservative estimated gross profit figure in preparing current monthly statements and the figure 33.3% was decided upon.

The first Planned Profit Program report indicated that the new owner was correct in his statement that the store was operating at a profit. It was, but increased inventory investment in the past several months and mounting accounts receivable totals had absorbed current profits. By the time the February report was completed, the benefits of remedial moves taken in the wake of the cash flow analysis program were beginning to show up. The February analysis looked like this:

Cash Flow Analysis

Depreciation (non-cash expense item)	$ 266.00
Operating Profit (before taxes)	$1,958.99
Inventory Reduction	$4,079.72
Accounts Receivable Reduction	$1,065.03
Total Available Cash	$7,369.74

Disposition

Accounts Payable Reduction	$3,000.00
Increase in Bank Balance	$4,369.74
	$7,369.74

During the month of March, progress continued, and the April analysis reflects more of the same. Inventories were better balanced and turnover improved. Accounts receivable were lower and more current.

The store was on a current basis and discounting all supplier statements with on-time payments. A payment of $5,000 had been made on the seller's note and the bank balance was substantial and quite sufficient to handle the Federal income tax payment due on the 15th of that month.

Here then is a brief case history of the benefits of monitoring cash flow and properly supervising the basic management controls.

The new store owner now has a feeling of confidence and has some clearly defined objectives and programs working to attain them. While the subject store is operating profitably, it can do better in this area, too. Even a cursory review of the operating expense items will reveal this fact to the experienced or practiced eye.

The Subject "A" store is simply one example of an existing operation and how the program outlined in this chapter aided in the solution of problems which, if ignored, would have inevitably led to failure.

There are many such examples in every market throughout America and the problems are not confined to new, relatively inexperienced management.

In every market, including the ones you service, you will find one or more additional examples. These are stores and customers that can be salvaged through the constructive application of a Planned Profit Program.

The results will be worth a large expenditure of thought, patience, time and effort on the part of your Financial Services Manager.

The Financial Services Manager's role in the future bears little resemblance to the "after the fact" Credit Manager's collection efforts, whose interest is only in getting the money and not salvaging a customer.

The Financial Service Manager's role is to salvage customers, improve management and create a strong customer base for his company.

Here are the Planned Profit Program work sheets on Subject "A" Store, followed by a sample arrangement confirmation letter, the substance of which may be altered to fit the factual circumstances of any problem account.

Prepare a confirmation letter in all instances to be dated and signed by the problem customer who retains the original letter and return the copy bearing his signature to you for your files.

Such a letter:

- becomes a definite commitment as to time and amount of payment
- it establishes venue at the supplier's county of residence — an advantage in the event things do not work out and litigation develops
- finally and most importantly, it commits the customer to a program requiring the preparation of forms reflecting basic operating controls. He now has a tool in his hand that will make him a better manager with a little helpful guidance and support
- in the event of a lapse in the preparation of monthly reports, a brief note or telephone call from the Financial Services Manager, referencing the agreement, will promptly get things back on the track again.

In this example, our customer had the ability to generate an adequate sales volume with merchandise realistically and competitively priced, deriving a normal gross profit with expenses well controlled resulting in a monthly operating profit of approximately $500 to as high as $2,500 before taxes.

The store's problem was inability to control inventory investment and failure to maintain current receivables.

Within a month the source of the inventory control problem was identified as were the sources of the store's collection problems.

Regarding the matter of inventory control, a recently employed lady in charge of the Cosmetic Department, including the buying function, was an excellent cosmetician and an effective saleslady, but not a buyer. With little regard for the investment involved, she filled the cases of her Cosmetic Department with numerous fragrance and treatment lines, each item stocked in depth. The Department's excessive inventory investment was steadily increasing each month. This was corrected by placing a limit on monthly purchases at 40% of department sales, and requiring the manager to approve all purchase orders by initialling them before mailing.

Accounts receivable were a two-fold problem:

1. Accounts were not opened with the proper procedure
2. Statements were not being mailed on time.

Referring to 1, when an account is opened for a new customer it is desirable that a careful, well thought out procedure be followed. In addition to the usual routine credit check and credit form use, the customer should be told, "Mrs. Jones, I have noticed you in the store often as a cash customer. We do offer charge account accommodations for shopping convenience. Our statements are mailed on the last day of each month and are payable upon receipt—in no case later than the 5th of the month. This requirement is necessitated by the fact that I must pay supplier's bills by the 10th of the month. Failing in this, I would lose the cash discount available and would have to raise my prices and it is my intention and desire to give my customers the best possible value at the lowest prices based on my cost." Make a little production out of opening an account with emphasis on the fact that this convenience is available only upon a prompt payment understanding. Any presentation that includes the importance of or the essential nature of prompt payment is a good procedure to follow in opening an account.

Contrast the above procedure with the following:

Mrs. Jones comes in and buys an item, an alarm clock for example, and she hands the item and a ten dollar bill to the clerk or store manager who pushes the ten dollar bill back over the counter to the customer with the comment "How about putting this on the books for you?" Here the man has money in hand and hands it back; there is no discussion of terms. The customer's impression is that this store has plenty of money and besides, it must make an awful lot of money on all those prescriptions.

At bill paying time, when the house payment is made, all utilities are paid, insurance premiums, school tuitions, etc., and the money runs out before the bills are paid, Mrs. Jones tosses the pharmacy bill back in the drawer for payment next month, along with the doctor's bill. The doctor owns the biggest house in the neighborhood and the pharmacist doesn't need his money any more than the doctor, so let these bills ride.

The proper procedure in opening an account is the first step in the collection effort.

The problem mentioned in 2 was handled by setting up a monthly statement preparation procedure by the wholesaler's computer program with statements prepared and delivered each month to the retailer for prompt mailing. An analysis of accounts by age was included in this program.

Mr. Jesse H. Jones described the Credit Manager's position as a very uncomplicated job, adding that he must have the affirmative answers to only two questions before the decision-making process takes place. These questions are:

1. Can he (the customer) pay?
2. Will he (the customer) pay?

The Financial Services Manager of tomorrow will add another dimension with this question; What can be done to help him pay?

See Chapter 9, "A New Concept in Credit Management."

The Monthly Analysis of Operations and the Planned Profit Program for Customers are essentially the same retail management aid, cash flow tracing programs. The same program is known by different names in different sections of the country. In one area of the country, one out of every ten customers serviced is or has been on one of these programs.

RESULTS

Credit losses dropped and reserve for bad debt requirements declined but, more importantly, strong, better than average managed stores exist in the market which forms the foundation of today's and tomorrow's sales volume sources. The Financial Services Manager has, by his constructive work with customers, laid a foundation for continued sales growth in the 1980's. This is healthy sales growth in strong, viable, profitable, well managed stores, the owners of which know how to avoid becoming a credit problem and incurring a possible credit loss. They know from experience, the value of the Monthly Analysis of Operations program and the advantages of consistent use of the Planned Profit Program For Customers.

Figure 8-3 illustrates both sides of the form put to use in this program that builds strong, loyal customers.

THE PLANNED PROFIT PROGRAM

(AN ANALYSIS OF MONTHLY BUSINESS)

Name of Store	Location	Month	Year

Charge Sales	$	
Cash Sales		

	AMOUNT	Your %	Av. %
Net Sales for Month TOTAL $			
Cost of Sales (Est.)			
Gross Profit (Est.)			

EXPENSES	AMOUNT	Your %	Av. %
Proprietor's Withdrawals $			
Employees' Salaries			
Rent			
Heat			
Light & Power			
Taxes & Licenses			
Insurance			
Interest			
Repairs			
Delivery			
Advertising			
Miscellaneous			
Depreciation			
Bad Debts Charged Off			
Telephone			

	AMOUNT	Your %	Av. %
Operating Expenses for Month TOTAL $			
Operating Profit or Loss			
Other Income (Discounts, etc.)			
Net Profit or Loss for Month			

Total Purchases $	
Accounts Payable, Total	
Notes Payable, Total	
Accounts Receivable, Total	
Bank Balance	

INSTRUCTIONS: Fill in only AMOUNT of Sales for Month, AMOUNT of each item of expense applicable in your operations, other income, and your total purchases for month, listing accounts payable, receivable, and bank balance and notes payable as of the end of the month. The form will be completed and returned to you promptly with a memorandum setting out any constructive comments that appear in order.

Form 4

ANOTHER CUSTOMER SERVICE FURNISHED WITHOUT CHARGE BY

Figure 8-3 (front)

BASIC OPERATING CONTROLS

In order to make the most efficient use of capital, it is imperative that an operating statement, preferably based on a Trial Balance, be prepared each month, and that this operating statement or "Analysis of Monthly Business" be analyzed so that management is in a position to trace earnings into increased inventory, reduced accounts and/or notes payable, increased accounts receivable, or into the bank. The preservation and disposition of profit is as essential as the ability to develop it.

Accounting records are a necessary management tool. An operating statement should be prepared monthly, using a conservative estimated gross profit figure as a basis between inventory periods. Without proper buying control inventories quickly become excessive, resulting in "lazy" investment dollars. Failure to control your accounts receivable investment can result in unnecessary losses as well as contribute to a slow capital turn. Operating expenses are difficult to control and a monthly check will keep the cost of doing business headed in the right direction.

Briefly reviewed here are the fundamental controls:

1. *Control sufficient sales volume* to sustain operating costs and develop a profit.
2. *Control your gross profit figure* with realistic pricing schedules, care in handling merchandise and money, and the avoidance of "leaks."
3. *Control operating expense.* Figure your percentages and compare with the industry average or your last year averages.
4. *Control your inventory investment.* Compare purchases each month with estimated cost of sales.
5. *Control your accounts receivable investment.* Compare with balances outstanding at close of previous month.

Preserve your earnings in the form of cash, and trace them *each month* into:

1. Increased inventory.
2. Reduced accounts and notes payable.
3. Increased accounts receivable.
4. Into the bank.

Remember, in this business what you have is not so important; it is what you are able to do with what you have that counts.

Figure 8-3 (back

9

A NEW CONCEPT IN CREDIT MANAGEMENT: MAXIMIZING THE FULL POTENTIAL OF THE CREDIT FUNCTION

A positive role for your financial services manager: long range help for the sales department.

THE CHALLENGE

Business enterprises, as a rule, have poorly used the time and abilities of their Credit Manager. The problem is that his role has been regarded as a negative one—a collector of debt—a man interested only in "getting the money." Regarded in some companies as a detriment or retardation to sales he becomes, in the role of the Financial Services Manager, a constructive force in building strong, healthy customers who respect his judgment, seek his advice and usually cooperate fully with him in generating and preserving earnings to apply on store indebtedness.

How is this transition accomplished?
How does it work?
What are the results?
What to do?

Rewrite your Credit Manager's job description and while at it, give him a new title, Financial Services Manager, one that better describes his new duties. See Figure 9-1.

The sample Financial Services Manager's job description given here is quite broad and includes many duties often assigned to the Credit Manager in small companies or smaller divisions of a large multi-division operation. Supervision of the Accounting Department, Office Management and other confining routine duties are to be avoided where possible so with these thoughts in mind, prepare an appropriate and practical job description for your Financial Services Manager. Keep in mind that his primary duties require:

- customer contacts
- that he function as a consultant to customers
- that he prepare Monthly Analysis of Operations or Planned Profit Program reports for those customers participating in these programs and write the required letters of analysis each month that accompany these reports
- that he handle "Design and Merchandising Department" contracts, notes and other essential papers
- that he spend a reasonable amount of time in the field, contacting customers on a planned schedule. These visits will include prompt paying customers as well as delinquent ones in need of his help.

Remember that his new role is that of a positive force in building better customers and improving customer relations and goodwill.

This is not "blue sky." We have the experience, many case histories and the arithmetic to prove it.

RESULTS

Subject Company "B" revised the job title (Credit Manager to Financial Services Manager), revised duties and responsibilities to correspond to the new concept in credit management and in all divisions, the Financial Services Manager became a sound, constructive member of the division management team. See specific results at the conclusion of this chapter.

Accounts previously not serviced because of being regarded as bad credit risks were helped to more successful operational levels and high volume catagories. Accounts, long serviced on a prompt paying basis which had begun to slip, were salvaged and headed back in the right direction because some temporary or transitory problem or perhaps even a chronic one or a combination of problems were identified and constructively handled in time to salvage an outlet for merchandise.

FINANCIAL SERVICES MANAGER

I. BASIC FUNCTION

He will be responsible for and handle all credit matters, supervise the Divisional accounting department, be expected to regularly contact all to whom he will offer our services.

II. DUTIES AND RESPONSIBILITIES

Within the limits of authorized Corporation policies, procedures, programs, and budgets, the Financial Services Manager will be responsible for:

1. Complete charge of all forms of credit and all matters pertaining to it; while he will invariably consult with the Divisional Manager, he will make the final decision on credit.

2. Working closely with the Design and Merchandising Department in drawing up contracts, in filing financing statements and in handling other legal papers, etc., and in passing on credit and terms allowed. The filing of such statements indicates that the company has a valid security agreement.

3. Supervision of the Division Accounting Department and the performance of its functions; hiring, firing and training of personnel, in consultation with the Division Manager. Will act also as Office Manager where such action does not conflict with other duties, or, if another is Office Manager, will supervise that person who will report directly to him.

4. Regularly contact customers in their stores, where he will thank those who habitually discount their bills, handle credit matters where needed, and will explain and offer to all customers such free financial services as monthly statement analysis, advice on leases, store locations, rentals, etc., consultation on other forms of financial matters, etc.

5. Keeping an up-to-date file, containing all pertinent information, on all Division accounts, to aid in making proper decisions for credit extension, special dating, ownership of new stores, etc.

6. Advising promptly both Division and Field Sales Managers of information he has obtained which may be helpful to them.

7. Appearing at all house sales meetings to advise and instruct the salesmen on credit problems and proper handling of them.

8. Assisting General Office staff with information obtained in the field, suggestions and advice on customer services and customer relations.

9. Supplementing efforts of Division and Field Sales Managers in extending and cementing trade and public relations.

10. Making special surveys as requested by the Division Manager or in handling special assignments as directed.

Figure 9-1

III. RELATIONSHIPS

The Financial Services Manager will establish and maintain the following relations and be accountable to the Division Manager for them.

1. Division Manager
    a. He is accountable to this executive for proper interpretation and fulfillment of his functions, responsibilities and authority, and relationships.
    b. As delegated in the job description or elsewhere in writing, he is final authority, after proper consultation with Managers on all credit decisions.

2. Department Heads

    He works closely with all, especially the Field Sales Manager, and cooperates in every way possible.

3. Other Members of Management

    He will coordinate his efforts with theirs toward the goals of the Corporation and stand ready at all times to render them assistance and advice; and call on them for assistance and advice as he deems necessary.

4. With Persons Outside the Corporation

    He will establish such relationship as he and the Division Manager deem advisable with representatives of other companies, associations, vendors, customers, the Government and the Public.

Fig 9-1 cont.

You may say, "So what's new about 'work out' credit problems? Jesse Jones collected fifty billion dollars on that basis for the Reconstruction Finance Corporation." Fine, but do you know how he did it? All of that money, an unprecedented delinquent indebtedness collection job, had to come from earnings of businesses with previous records of operating losses. The principles employed were simple, they work today and they will work tomorrow. Operating information has to be used to generate and preserve profit to apply on debt. When you ask a customer to enter upon a "past due" debt reduction program, you are asking him to make payments over and above merchandise replacement costs and it is important to know where the money comes from. In fact, this information is essential.

You can work constructively with a problem account only when you gain his confidence; get into his records, provide an adequate system of accounting if none exists, show your customer how to prepare and use his records for management purposes. Future stakes are so great and the monies involved so substantial that slipshod methods often used and considered reasonably adequate in the past just won't work any more. Help your customers to recognize this fact, to adjust and grow with you.

Delinquent accounts increase your equity investment requirements, reduce R.O.I., and constitute potential losses.

Adequate accounting records, current balance sheets and operating statements plus a thorough understanding of operating problems and definite programs for remedial action can be brought to your customer's banker for review and discussion in arranging for short-term loan assistance. If your customer uses one bank and regularly deposits the proceeds of his sales and collections in that bank, he probably carries a very respectable balance, considering the "float factor" on his own accounts payable checks and the banker knows this and probably considers the account a desirable one. Teach your customer how to use his bank, what preparations should be made in advance of an appointment for the discussion of a loan application. If the banker is convinced that the applicant knows his business, maintains adequate records and knows how to use and interpret them, that he has a good knowledge of his problem, that it is temporary and that a practical solution or program has been devised to remedy the situation and provide the funds necessary for an orderly liquidation of the bank debt as agreed, he will in most instances be favorably inclined to approve a reasonable short-term loan.

Banks make loans as well as receive deposits and pay checks drawn on those deposits as well as render other services. Many small merchants do not seem to realize this fact and they look to suppliers for financial assistance. If they consider their bank as a source of financial assistance, they usually enter the bank, hat in hand, with no records and no presentation plans; only an attitude of combined embarrassment and humiliation. Many need to be taught how to use their bank services. To teach a customer the proper approach and a few basic "do's and don'ts" is to help that customer on the road to maturity in handling his business financial responsibilities. He will find that his banker is not so much concerned with what he has as he is with what he is able to do with what he has. If he can tell his story convincingly, has the aritmetic to support it and impresses the banker favorably as a man who is competent in his field of business, who has identified his problem correctly and has the capacity to repay a loan on the terms agreed upon, the banker will help. This is one of his services—perhaps the principal one.

A few words of caution:

- request only the amount needed
- make the payment schedule well within the ability to pay
- always make payments *on or before due dates*, never as much as even one day later than the due date
- visit the banker from time to time and keep him informed regarding your progress; just a brief visit, at regular but infrequent intervals, will suffice.

To teach a customer how to use his bank is in itself a constructive service and there is more need for it than you think.

Now for some specific suggestions for you to consider and the results of Subject Company "B" mentioned:

SUGGESTIONS

1. Start by asking your Credit Manager to prepare a brief job description of his job as he understands it to be and give it to you. You may suggest some broad outline of the form in which you want the job description.

2. Tell your Credit Manager that the title "Financial Services Manager" may be a better descriptive term for the job he will be expected to do in the future.

3. Tell him what is expected of him. If he succeeds, reward him at a level commensurate with his contribution to *increased* company earnings.

RESULTS

SUBJECT COMPANY "B" upon conversion to the Financial Services Manager concept

- increased sales
- reduced credit losses charged to reserve for bad debts
- reduced accounts receivable investment
- eliminated reserve for bad debt charges in some divisions; reduced the percentage of reserve provided in relation to sales in others
- increased operating profit
- increased company R.O.I.
- strengthened the company's market position.

The answers to credit and collection problems are no longer where they used to be. The increasing pressures of stronger and more demanding collection letters simply bear no relevance to the constructive handling of future credit and collection problems. The day of the "tough credit man" is over. The period of the builder in the field of Financial Service Management is just beginning. It is a much more demanding role. His probing must be deeper, his access to facts more complete. His primary interest will be in salvaging and building customers. If a cooperative effort is impossible and his collection efforts result in a "rob Peter to pay Paul" procedure, he will feel a sense of failure. Just getting the money from an account that passes up one creditor to pay another simply "changes the place but doesn't relieve the pain" — this is failure. The Financial Services Manager of tomorrow is interested in success.

As we have noted, Jesse H. Jones said; "The Credit Manager's job is not a complicated one. It is actually rather simple. The Credit Manager must have an affirmative answer to only two basic basic questions in making his decisions. Those questions are:

1. Can he pay?
2. Will he pay?

Later, this premise was modified to add this dimension:

- If he can't pay, what can we do to help him with his problems to improve his operations so that he can pay?
- If we can solve the problems, generate profit and monitor the cash flow, the "Can he pay" question is out of the picture. If the money is there and he can pay, there are many useful, fair and equitable procedures to follow, if necessary, to see that he will pay.

These modifications lift the concept of the Credit Manager's job into the Financial Services Manager field of operation.

This concept goes far beyond the two primary questions of "Can he pay?" and "Will he pay?" and Jesse H. Jones was among the first to visualize and to successfully use credit management as a productive tool not only to collect money, but to help others use the money they control more wisely and more efficiently. This was the key to his R. F. C. success story. It cast a long shadow into the future and became a new formula for successful credit management.

This is where the action is today and where the opportunities will continue to exist during the next decade. Old concepts, old approaches and negative procedures never did work well in the Credit Department. They won't work at all now. There just isn't that much time available anymore to bother with them. Gear up your Credit Department to render meaningful, constructive services in the field of Financial Services Management. Add a new dimension to your operations in an area that has for years been the least cultivated of management talents and skills.

You have reviewed case history results. They are good. Do not these results justify "tinkering with the wheel," probing and exploring how it can be made to work better for you? It is what we are able to do with what we have that counts.

The Financial Services Manager is tomorrow's replacement for yesterday's Credit Manager.

10

PICKING THE BEST QUALIFIED PEOPLE: THE EMPLOYEE PERFORMANCE EVALUATION FILE

A formula and procedure for selecting superior people for promotion or new job assignments: remove most recent impression problems, good or bad, which may not be typical of overall performance; take the long look and do it accurately. These techniques work and provide answers to other problems relative to employee promotion and selection.

THE CHALLENGE

In selecting management personnel, objectivity and the availability of facts are essential in all considerations. How to avoid judgments of personnel performance based on most recent activity or some recent event, good or bad, and not typical of the general performance of the employee under consideration, constitutes a very real problem—one involv-

135

ing fairness, not only to the employee involved in the consideration, but to the company itself.

How to properly evaluate initiative, ability to cope, decision making capacity, perceptiveness, how well the employee stands up under pressure, his or her initiative, his or her weaknesses—all of these factors should be known and they can be known and considered at the right time.

THE SOLUTION

The Chief Executive Officer maintains a confidential Employee Performance Evaluation File on every individual to whom consideration for advancement in management is a possibility. Every employee knows, of course, that the file exists; it is not a "big brother is looking over your shoulder" thing at all, but rather a carefully kept record of performance which is fair, accurate and desirable to have. The file contains a record of all successes, jobs well done, experimentations suggested, new ideas that have helped the company and have succeeded in becoming innovations. All are recorded to no one else's credit, nor are the failure and shortcomings known to management.

It works this way:

- management keeps in a confidential, locked file cabinet, a complete set of personal memoranda on individual employee performances
- from time to time as the performance of an employee, good or poor, comes to the attention of management in the normal course of day-to-day business, a brief, handwritten memorandum is prepared outlining the known facts or the events that have transpired. He then dates, initials and drops it into the appropriate employee file. This information plus any trade journal news item clippings concerning business activity and industry organization positions to which the employee has been elected and his accomplishments in those positions, etc. are also placed in the file
- all of these files are pulled, their contents arranged in chronological order and reviewed for all individuals being considered as candidates to fill a new or vacant management position
- each candidate is then personally interviewed and the file's contents reviewed with that person
- the object, of course, is to select the best qualified man based on known facts about him and his accomplishments and possible capabilities.

Such a file can be helpful in administering job description, job evaluation, merit rating programs at quarterly, six-month or annual intervals, depending upon the frequency required for preparing merit rating reports. Hearsay, rumors, questionable and unverified reports about an employee are meticulously avoided.

In this constructive management technique, I have taken a page from John Edgar Hoover's instructions. Hoover was the best administrator with whom I have ever been associated—in business or government.

RESULTS

The President and Chairman of the Board of a successful multi-million dollar, publicly owned company was selected in this manner. He has also just completed a term as national President of his industry trade organization. He is a product of the Employee Performance Evaluation File, as are several Regional Vice-Presidents and many other key personnel of the same company.

In dealing with people, you can't always put the results down in numbers but the performances of the companies under the guidance of individuals who are the products of this management evaluation and selection technique are good and are improving.

I cannot recall any instance of unfavorable results when leadership is chosen on a factual basis consisting of broad based past performance records and experience. You cannot always tell what a person will do in the future simply by reviewing past performance. Few unpleasant surprises result when you know in advance of appointment what kind of behavior patterns have developed under conditions similar to those the appointee will face in his or her new assignment.

This is simply one prime example of results that are known. There are many others in manufacturing, retail and wholesale distribution. The technique works by eliminating decisions based on most recent performance impressions which are not always typical of overall performance.

Since your company's largest investment in time and money is in people, doesn't it make sense to objectively monitor, develop and maximize this resource by careful selection of the best qualified people based on his or her own record of handling responsibilities over a period of months or years? This record is certainly desirable and useful. It is available only if you keep it.

One additional procedural recommendation:

When you pull a file and set up its contents in chronological order, prepare a memorandum and attach the contents to that. Try to chart trend lines of mistake or error frequencies, as well as positive factors. If recent performance is consistently improved, this trend is, of course, significant.

Ask the person being interviewed for comments or observations pertaining to each entry on the memorandum. Is the person forthright, defensive or antagonistic? Does he or she question the accuracy of any item listed? Check it out. Pay attention to the "vibes."

In the lower left hand side of the memorandum on the last sheet have this line typed:

"I have reviewed the contents of this memorandum with John Doe and my initial below indicates that I am aware of its contents but do not necessarily agree with every statement set out."

You, the interviewer, should then date and initial the right hand side at the conclusion of the interview.

In addition to the primary objective of making the best possible appointments based on known past performance factors, there is an added bonus. Your people know that you are making every effort to be objective and fair in your decisions concerning personnel selection. Failing to receive the appointment, there will be some who will not like your decision but they will know that you did go to great length to scan every available fact before the decision process was concluded and this makes for good morale and generally engenders broad support of and cooperation with the person selected.

People do things for their own reasons. This procedure gives them reasons to support the person selected for the new responsibilities. This can become each person's own reason for cooperation.

You have:

- been objective
- fair
- afforded a degree of recognition to each person interviewed
- indicated an interest in the personal growth and opportunity for advancement of all persons interviewed. This is a continuing interest known to each person on which a memorandum was prepared
- provided incentives for better performance.

All of these things are motivators and/or satisfiers in themselves. Since business is the "doings of people" and motivated people do things better, you have used a personal selection method that does more than help you select the right person for this particular responsibility. You have used it to motivate others. And that in itself is a positive value of considerable proportions.

Negatives can be avoided by:

- confining your part of the interview to a series of quiet spoken pertinent questions
- avoid giving an impression of preference in any way
- avoid any reference or comment regarding any other person or persons interviewed or to be interviewed.

Yours is a scanning procedure; you get an overview of qualified people. Commitments and discussions, if they are to take place at all, come later on an individual basis. This provides opportunities to review areas of strength as well as weaknesses, to discuss what improvements are desired and will be looked for in order to improve qualifications. People want to know that. Tell them.

PART IV
EQUITY SOURCES

Corporate Planning and Financial Planning: Appraisal, Development and the Use of People

11

COPING WITH PROBLEMS OF REORGANIZATION: OPERATIONAL STRUCTURE

How to structure operations, following merger or acquisition, for best results: do's and don't's that pay off.

THE CHALLENGE

After acquisition or merger, an immediate and high priority consideration is how to structure the operating organization for the best results.

Planning the operational structure for a newly merged enterprise combining two or more previously independent operations involves two problem areas requiring consideration and decisions at the outset of the combined operation activity. These problems areas are:

1. Whether or not to regionalize operations, move to regional management responsibility and
2. The consideration of separating operations responsibility and sales responsibility with separate and clearly defined chains of command from the division level to top supervision or management in each area.

Having been operationally involved in a number of mergers and acquisitions and having been in a position to observe the results, primarily in the distribution field, not only of my own experiences but that of others as well when these decisions were being considered and the operating structure set up, the results of affirmative decisions in both of these areas are well known to me. They have, in the main, been unsatisfactory in the results attained.

Consideration will be given separately to each of these two problem areas.

1. REGIONALIZATION OF MANAGEMENT

- To begin with, when you regionalize you build in another layer of management cost, a cost that did not exist before merger.
- Does the regionalization of management speed up or slow down the promptness with which critical customer service problems are handled?
- Is regional management an insulator or a conduit between top management and what is really happening at the division level?
- Is your regional management comprised of better decision makers than your division management?
- Do your division managers tend to abdicate their decision-making responsibilities when they refer urgent matters needing prompt decisions to their regional managers?
- Do regional management people tend to look up to top management for approval or down to division management to serve and help? The direction of this attention is significant and critical to constructive supervision.
- Where are the problems that really count? Are they between division management and regional supervision; regional supervision and top management; or are the problems between customers and servicing divisions that immediately affect sales and profits, the ones that your operation should be geared to handle? If you live in the real world of day-to-day competitive business activity you will know or at least have a "gut feeling" that there are no more important problems to handle effectively and promptly than those involving customers.

This series of questions is not a statement of a problem but rather questions that constitute the roots of a problem and a serious one. The wrong answers to these questions can impede company progress and adversely affect profits.

SOLUTION

The most constructive, and therefore correct, answer to the consideration of regionalization is:

- DON'T DO IT
- encourage and require your division managers to make and live with the results of their own decisions, made within stated company policies.

RESULTS

Minimum regional management structuring or none at all, tends to:

- strengthen division management capacity to perform
- be less costly in terms of salary structure
- speed up problem handling, decision making and remedial handling of problems in the sensitive area of customer relations.

In summary, better and more effective management results and it is less costly.

In this section of the chapter up to this point we have given primary consideration to the field of distribution; that is, the wholesaler or distributor operation servicing retail customers.

Regionalization in many manufacturer marketing operations is desirable and works well. The basic circumstances are quite different. Usually the factory itself is some distance from sales territories serviced and close supervision of a national sales force can be attained more effectively through regional sales supervision. So in the manufacturer area, we are talking in terms of regionalization of a sales force only and not operations as is the case when we consider distribution structures.

2. SEPARATION OF OPERATION AND SALES RESPONSIBILITIES

You may say, "Who would make such a severance decision and why?"

For a manufacturer, the separation of operations and sales is logical and it works effectively. Here we have research and manufacturing, and marketing or sales. The demarkation line is clear and logical. Salesmen do not relate to the manufacturing operation. Production and sales are logically completely separate operations. Both areas are accountable for performance directly or indirectly to top management.

Salesmen are not employed by and are not accountable for their performance to the factory manager or superintendent of production, but rather to the Marketing Manager or General Sales Manager.

In the field of distribution, the separation of operations and sales responsibility does not work. Why?

Salesmen are employees of the division to which they are assigned. They perform other duties in addition to sales, for which they are accountable to the Division Manager.

The Sales Department originates all sales programs and assigns these promotions to division salesmen for execution. Quotas are set by sales management and results of all sales performances are supervised and evaluated by the General Sales Manager or Marketing Manager.

It is in the area of promotional selling that differences between Division Managers and Sales Managers most frequently have their origin.

A Division Manager may on occasion decline to go along with a proposed sales promotion in his division and for a very good reason which should be communicated at once to the General Sales Manager or Marketing Manager.

Example:

A sundry sales promotion conceived for sale over a very large market area, may have as one of the promotional items a quantity of rain umbrellas at a good price; an appropriate promotional item in some markets, but not in Tucson or Phoenix, Arizona, where rain generally is a rarity. It would be a constructive service for managers in these areas to immediately contact Sales Management and ask that some other more suitable promotional item be substituted for these two divisions, if possible.

A word of caution—if frequency of sales promotion item rejection seems to center around one or two Division Managers, they should be called into the General Office and individually told by top management that the situation exists and will not be tolerated; full support of all sales programs is expected of all Division Managers.

Future exceptions will be rare and must be exceptionally well-founded.

In the distribution field, since salesmen are employees of the division to which they are assigned, the following duties and activities of salesmen are usually subject to Division Management supervision:

- reporting for work in the territory assigned, each day and on time
- making daily customer calls on schedule
- handling adjustments
- reporting service complaints
- return goods handling
- reporting significant changes in the territory such as changes of ownership, new store locations, available or new stores
- any changes or improvement in competitive delivery schedules
- personal conduct of salesmen in territory
- reporting quality of division service such as accuracy of order filling, omission rates, dependable, on time delivery schedules, etc.
- receipt and return of samples
- other division and customer service related duties.

The Division Manager follows sales results himself and supports the General Sales Manager or Marketing Manager in all of his programs and objectives for his division and for the company in the area of promotional selling.

RESULTS

- Closer day to day supervision of all territory salesmen
- Division Managers remain interested in sales, feeling that increasing sales is the first management control towards increased profits
- Better promotional selling results are obtained
- Better division profit performance results.

In the distribution field an operating division is a profit center. Sales and services are both integral parts of the same operation. How can you hold a division manager responsible for division profits when you remove responsibility for sales, the top line of his operating statement, where it all begins?

Operations management attitude develops along this line; there is nothing wrong with this operation or this division that increased sales volume would not correct.

The Sales department takes the position that their problem is poor service, high omission rates, errors in order filling. With the right kind of operations, sales would be no problem.

So here we have a combative situation developing where cooperation and mutual support is essential.

In distribution, the division manager must have overall responsibility for both sales and service or operations for best results.

GOING PUBLIC AND OTHER FORMS OF PERMANENT FINANCING

The pros and cons of going public, a critical and costly decision. Some alternatives to think about.

Management/ownership of a private business, faced with the following conditions, might consider going public:

- expansion beyond its capital structure to handle a growing business, or
- an inheritance tax problem involving the estate of a major shareholder in the business, or
- a major shareholder, active in management, wishing to retire and diversify his investment, make his estate more liquid, and its assets more readily marketable.

These reasons for going public seem to predominate although there are many others that could be listed. Your reason for considering going public or arranging other forms of permanent financing may be none of these.

THE CHALLENGE

Whatever its source, the problem itself is (a) the marketability of stock in a privately held corporation, usually, management owned or controlled, or (b) the need for some kind of permanent financing arrangements.

SOLUTION

An investment banker is approached with the statement, "we want to go public." Once the matter is explored, more often than not, management has simply recognized the need for some move to provide permanent capital.

In some instances, an initial public offering to provide the capital needed is the answer. There are other approaches that may be more desirable.

Selling shares publicly involves some degree of change in the operating characteristics of the company, perhaps minimal, perhaps fairly major. Operating in the publicly owned world cannot be too difficult, as indicated by the number of companies of all sizes and characters operating this way. Thus, going public should be considered as one of the financing alternatives—but only one of them.

The most basic of the other alternatives is the sale of long term debt. The benefits of this approach are obvious:

- There is no effect on the ownership of the issuer
- Interest expense is a pre-tax charge
- Even the cost of securing the long term debt arrangement is an amortizable expense
- The procedure involved in obtaining funds is fast and simple compared to other methods of securing permanent capital
- The size and terms of the issue can be tailored to suit the particular circumstances.

Although the debt must be repaid, repayment is stretched out over a number of years. There are negatives.

- The very benefits of this method may result in many others seeking to use this type of financing and your company may find that it cannot obtain or secure funds on any reasonable basis.
- If you do qualify, you will be subject to indenture restrictions which can prove to be burdensome, particularly if you wish to change the course of your business activities.
- While the money does have to be repaid, there are usually restrictions and/or penalties imposed in connection with early repayment.

While no financing method is suitable for every corporation or other form of business enterprise, the placement of long-term debt has such broad application that corporate executives should be aware of the basic considerations involved in this approach to financing and investigate the matter thoroughly with the aid of a competent investment banker with experience and a successful record in this field.

There are instances in which debt financing is unavailable, impractical, or undesirable.

PRIVATE SALE OF EQUITY

A second alternative is equity, but not a public offering, the private sale of equity! This procedure, of course, involves bringing in one or more new stockholders. In some instances there may be an individual who would like to invest in and take an active interest in the operations of your company. As an example, a retired, successful businessman might prefer this to a more passive investment. The amount of capital available from one individual is normally limited, so this approach is usually suitable only for smaller operations. Generally, several investors participate in a private equity financing. These investors can range from individuals to corporate entities specializing in private equity investments. A basic benefit of this alternative is that capital is permanent. At the same time, this type of investor usually wants an idea as to when and how he will be in a position to liquidate his investment. For this reason, this method is most widely used when there is an intention to make a public offering or merge with a public company in the not too distant future. Another limitation on private equity financing is the limited amount of availability relative to either private debt or public equity. On the positive side, this approach is fast, relatively inexpensive, and can be utilized to secure smaller amounts of capital.

It is a method lacking the broad application of private debt but very useful when the circumstances are right.

SALE AND LEASEBACK

The third approach is the sale and leaseback of physical assets, which combines features of both debt and equity. You sell your equity in the assets and you transfer any borrowings against the assets from a debt to a lease obligation. The principal limitation in this procedure is the availability in a given operation of assets suitable for this procedure. This method is most appropriate where the assets (buildings) are general purpose in nature. There are investors who specialize in this activity, and it can be a flexible source of capital for many businesses.

Other approaches to permanent financing are used much less often as they carry with them more business considerations.

One such approach is the acquisition of stock in a cash-rich private company. In many ways this is similar to a private equity financing with the added consideration as to the operating assets which come along with the cash. Obviously, there are a limited number of companies of this type which are around, much less available. As with any of the more unique transactions, one of this type requires care and a degree of luck, but a well executed acquisition of this type can accomplish the financing needs that exist and bring added benefits.

Closely akin is the acquisition of a publicly owned company with characteristics which allow your operation to remain the dominant force. If financing is your motivating factor, then the company being acquired should have either cash or assets which can and will be converted into cash. For you to remain the dominant force, the other company probably must be smaller or have little in the way of operating assets. Here again, you must evaluate the operating assets and you also will end up as a public company. This approach can bring you several significant benefits, but it needs to be considered with extreme care due to the many and diverse factors involved.

SALE OF A SUBSIDIARY, DIVISION OR PRODUCT LINE

A final approach to financing may not seem like financing at all and, while it is a common practice, it is usually carried out for reasons other than financing. This approach is the sale of an operating subsidiary, division or product line. A sale of this type is usually considered when:

1. the unit is not operating properly, or
2. it no longer fits the corporate approach.

However when financing is needed, the sale of an operating unit may be the least expensive, if not the only feasible approach available. Recognizing that this approach is contrary to much human nature, it is still a practical solution, worthy of careful, objective evaluation. It is simply a decision based on the consideration of what things you are willing to give up in order to make other things secure and, having made this judgment, having the tenacity to stay with it and carry it through to a successful conclusion.

There are naturally variations and combinations of all of these approaches, limited only by one's imagination. So, if permanent capital is a consideration, do not feel that there are no solutions if a public offering of equity is not appropriate.

Back to our first alternative, the public offering of equity. As stated, many corporations have utilized this approach, and most of them have lived comfortably with it since their initial offering. There are many benefits from public ownership but the corporation takes on a number of continuing responsibilities.

One of my associates characterized going public as like joining a country club in that, at the outset, the initiation fee looked like the big factor, but it was the monthly dues that became the bigger consideration. An initial public offering is involved and is an expensive undertaking but the continuing obligations incident to having public ownership are far more important and more demanding.

The first consideration is whether your company can make a public sale of equity at a given time. If not, whatever the reason may be, the exercise becomes academic. If it appears that a public sale can be accomplished on a reasonable basis, the next step is to project forward and analyze your own company in light of the many factors involved in continuing public ownership. In other words, do not let the enthusiasm involved in contemplating an initial public offering deter you from carefully considering the long range effects of becoming publicly held.

Once you are public, it is most difficult to revert to a private basis. This fact has been well illustrated by events in the 1974-1975 period, when several large corporations and some smaller ones attempted to go private. An unusual combination of investor emotions and regulatory decisions worked against the most seemingly fair approach.

Many corporations with stock selling substantially below book value in a depressed market, have bought their own shares in open market transactions, and in so doing, accomplished these results:

- reduced the number of shares outstanding
- increased the number of unissued shares held by the company as treasury stock
- decreased dividend liability
- a reduction in shares outstanding increased earnings per share (net after tax operating profits divided by number of shares outstanding).

There are some rules of thumb that do not apply under all circumstances but they are basic and worth remembering:

- the stock of a corporation earning 10% after taxes on investment generally sells or should sell at book value
- if earnings are 15% after taxes, the stock in a normal market (one that is not depressed or inflated) will usually sell for 150% of book value
- earnings of 20% after taxes will as a rule result in a market price of 200% of book value or twice the book value of the stock.

If, in a depressed market, a corporation's stock is selling for half of book value (for example, in utter disregard of earnings figures) that stock is an excellent buy by the corporation to hold as unissued treasury stock for obvious reasons. One proviso—that the financial position of the corporation permits this.

Despite these broad rules of thumb, the price of any stock is really determined by the price a buyer will pay for it and at what price a seller will sell it. It is a primary trading proposition, price being determined by seller and buyer agreement.

MAJOR CONSIDERATIONS FOR MANAGEMENT

One factor which often concerns management is control, or more specifically the loss threof. While there is some risk, it is far less than generally imagined. The public "buys" management and wants results, but has no interest in trying to run the business. The public investor feels that he can always sell his stock if he is dissatisfied with management. Also, control by management of the proxy machinery is a strong defense against any takeover attempt. Other specific arrangements such as issuing several classes or classifications of stock can work as a defense against raid or takeover attempts.

Another valid concern of management is disclosure. The registration statement covering the initial offering must contain considerable information relative to the company, but this is only the start. Detailed annual reports, and more limited quarterly reports, must be filed with the Securities and Exchange Commission. The proxy statement covering the annual meeting of stockholders must be filed with and approved by the Securities and Exchange Commission; other material should be made available to stockholders. Even where there is no questionable business about which to be concerned, management may be properly concerned about revealing such information as sales and profits by major product groups, which a competitor would find valuable.

Closely related to disclosure is the continuing cost, in time, effort and direct expense of preparing and distributing required filings with regulatory agencies as well as desirable information for stockholders. This represents a continuing, and not insignificant, expense related to having public stockholders.

Another concern of many managements relates to dealing with stockholders and the financial community. This concern may be only a fear of the unkonwn, or it may be a genuine problem. Most corporate executives thoroughly enjoy constructive meetings with shareholders and financial analysts. A conservative posture, letting the facts speak for themselves and the avoidance of overly optimistic predictions of future company performance, contributes to credibility and confidence.

DYNAMICS AFFECTING THE PRICE OF YOUR STOCK

One principal factor in public ownership is the degree of importance that is taken on by the quoted market price of your stock. The market price at any given moment is the value of your stock and, in turn, of the company, for almost every purpose short of the total sale of the company. Future equity and equity related financing relates to this market price; stock options are based on this price, acquisitions utilizing equity are based on this price, and on and on.

The price level of stock in the public market can prove quite frustrating to management. In some instances, corporate executives have a price, or more properly a price range, at which the stock of the company represents a reasonable value. More often than not, the market price is either above or below this range. If it is above the range, there is concern that the new purchaser may be paying too much. If the price is below the range, which seems to be the more prevalent situation, there is concern that the marketplace is not properly recognizing the merits of the company. This area thus represents another factor to be aware of in contemplating a public offering.

The factors which influence the market price are numerous and diverse. Basic are the operating results of the company, past, present and the outlook for the future. Also of importance are general market levels, investor interest in a given company's industry, cash dividends and even the nature of management's approach to financial public relations. Company officials should recognize that they will be learning more about the public market if the securities of their company trade publicly, even if these officials had prior experience with the stock market.

Other considerations may or may not be important. One example is cash dividends. Investors may talk about growth, but current income has great appeal. In this regard, keep in mind that the public stockholder receives no other compensations from the company. Another example is the matter of outside directors. The practice among public companies varies widely, but in many cases some representation from outside management proves desirable.

Earlier it was assumed that your company had the requisites which made feasible an initial public offering. What are these requisites, you may ask? Unfortunately, there are no hard and fast rules, but there are some guidelines. The first requisite is a receptive general market climate. A few offerings are possible in just about any market climate, but most are feasible only in a particular marketplace. This presents several problems. The markets, as gauged by the recognized averages, fluctuate in an irregular and unpredictable pattern. Interest in new issues tends to lag behind a rising market but also tends to hold up after the market averages turn lower. Even more unpredictable is the degree of marketplace interest in a given industry or type of company. Since the time from the decision to proceed on a public offering to the actual offering date is relatively long (four to six months as a general rule), being ready to offer when the marketplace is receptive requires careful planning, good advice and a fair measure of luck.

ESTABLISHING THE SIZE OF THE OFFERING

Companies of all sizes and shapes have successfully offered stock publicly, with the ones lacking strong fundamentals usually having caught a time of high interest in new offerings. Thus, any guidelines cannot relate to what is necessary for accomplishing a public offering but can only relate to what seems necessary to make a public offering which provides the basis for a market with reasonable depth and continuity. Regarding size, net after tax earnings of $500,000 seem minimum at the present time, and the $1,000,000 area is much more desirable. An offering of $2,500,000 is a desirable minimum, but $4,000,000 to $5,000,000 provides more assurance. As to the type of company, a record of steady increases in operating results will find more followers than a cyclical record. Also, the marketplace tends to prefer, among smaller companies, the ones with a strong pattern of growth over the solid, slow growth situation as there are plenty of solid, slow growth issues among large corporations. As noted before, various industries come into favor or fashion, and some drop out of fashion.

If the recommended minimums as to size seem large, be cautioned that in the public marketplace you will be competing for the investor's attention with the largest corporations. A resulting consideration is that public ownership entails some substantial expenses, many of which are more fixed than variable in nature. In giving consideration to an initial public offering, be certain that you understand what expenses will be paid by the sellers and receive a solid estimate of these expenses. Also, be sure you understand that a substantial portion of these expenses will be incurred before you secure a firm commitment; put another way, you will incur quite an expense even if the offering is never made.

One aspect of public offering which often is overlooked relates to the necessary prior planning. In many situations, matters are handled no differently whether or not a public offering is contemplated. In others though, the business is run in a manner totally appropriate to private ownership but which can prove detrimental to the basis of a public offering. One of the most common problem areas relates to the audits; audited financial statements with an unqualified opinion for three years are required in a filing. Some private companies may feel they do not need a full audit. However, it may prove difficult, if not impossible, for the auditors to remove a qualification, particularly if it relates to an area such as inventories. Another problem area can be dealings between the corporation on the one hand and its officers and directors on the other. Any such transaction during the previous three years must be disclosed, and even the most fair dealings can require substantial explanation. A third area relates to the operating record of the company including officer salaries, income tax policy and similar areas of decision.

Since each company is different, someone contemplating a public offering might do well to outline a registration statement to see if there are any activities which need adjustment to put the company in a better posture when an actual filing is made. Advice of legal counsel, accountants and even a reputable investment banker at an early date may minimize later problems.

For the third time—there are many benefits accruing from the public ownership of your stock—just be sure you are well aware of the obligation which goes along with these benefits.

13

FINANCIAL PLANNING AS PART OF CORPORATE PLANNING

*Avoid looking at your organization through the
narrow prism of financial targets. Keep the focus
on total corporate operating needs and goals.*

A discussion of financial planning may come about when the subject is really overall corporate planning. The two areas are certainly interrelated but it is important for management to recognize the true subject.

THE CHALLENGE

Unfortunately, sometimes the financial position of a corporation reaches the point whereby corporate decisions are dictated by financial considerations. This is an undesirable situation which can result from unanticipated circumstances, but more commonly results from shortcomings in total corporate financing planning. Hopefully your company will never reach this position, at least from lack of planning.

EXAMPLE

A case history illustrates how financial planning can lead to corporate planning. The company was a medium-sized regional company with a good operating history and an adequate financial position. The company had some ten stockholders, all employees, of whom two were dominant; one was an older man who was by far the largest stockholder, the second was a man just hitting his stride as a top operator. Management met with the company's accountants and lawyers, and then with a leading investment banking firm headquartered in the same city, to discuss going public. Out of these meetings came the realization by management that a number of alternatives were avaialable to them, so the two key individuals met again with representatives of the investment banking firm to take a broad look. The alternatives included:

1. continue to operate without significant change
2. make a public offering, with the intention of thereafter acquiring for stock similar operations in other cities in the region
3. make a public offering using the additional capital to accelerate internal growth
4. be acquired by and become an operating division of a national company in the same business
5. be acquired by a company headquartered in the same city with operations in related businesses but not this one.

The decision actually reached is not as important as the fact that each alternative was weighed from the aspects of what was best for the future operations of the business, what was best for the stockholders and employees, and what were the financial considerations. Management had reviewed not just the financial but also the operational and personnel factors and came to a thoughtful evaluation of the direction in which the company should move.

It is possible that any one of several of these alternatives would have worked out well, and the one chosen certainly did. The company decided upon alternative 4., acquisition by a national firm in the same business. Such a merger was accomplished, the consideration being the stock of the parent firm. Within one year the parent made an offering and these shareholders had the opportunity to include any amount of stock suitable to the needs and desires of the individual. The largest stockholder sold a good portion of his holding, allowing him to better diversify; the man who was just hitting his stride as a top operator moved into a position of increased responsibility in the parent firm. All in all, the decision reached was suitable in view of the factors present. Operating as a regional headquarters, the other shareholders found themselves managing a rapidly growing segment of the company. They gave up some independence, but this was not critical to these individuals.

This particular company had a unique opportunity in that so many viable alternatives were available at this particular time. This is not always the situation, yet upon examination any corporation at any given time may find it has available more alternatives than would first appear. Your decision may be to make no significant change, but you should be aware of the types of financing available and how alternative financing methods are an integral part of corporate planning. Many of these alternatives are outlined in the preceding chapter. There are others; see Chapter 17.

Financial planning may be relatively short term and be safe in a static growth situation.

Corporate planning takes into account all possible foreseeable changes. Considerations as to:

- how long to plan for
- defining objectives
- establishing a timetable
- estimating captial needs if objectives are met
- alternative sources of required capital
- acquisition and/or merger considerations.

14

OPERATIONAL USE OF SHORT RANGE MANAGEMENT BY OBJECTIVE: THE COMPANY PLAN

Implementing short range M-B-O: an operational approach, can you get where you want to go from here?

THE CHALLENGE

Plans for the future use of company resources are essential, notwithstanding the fact that no one can predict with certainty what events will transpire in the future. Company objectives must be defined if they are to be reached and comparative figures reflecting accomplishment to plan must be available at frequent intervals (monthly).

Part of the challenge is to arrive at realistic objectives—a company plan that is attainable but requires persistent best efforts in its accomplishment. We are speaking in terms of short-term operational profit planning—from year to year. The last and equally essential part of the challenge has to do with establishing a basis for rewarding accomplishment.

WHAT TO DO

"Five year plans" in current vogue throughout industry are of little practical, operational value. They are cumbersome and difficult to administer. Comparisons made over such a protracted period of time tend to lose operational meaning. It is recognized that the Chief Executive Officer and his Executive Committee as well as the Board of Directors must certainly give thought to and effectively plan for the future profitable use of shareholders' investments in the Company. They will concern themselves with five, ten fifteen, twenty, twenty-five year plans and even more extended programs or objectives unannounced as targets and regarded as general long-term considerations. However, the most practical "management by objective" tool is the one year Company plan or outline of annual Company objectives. Again, objectives must be realistic, difficult or high but attainable, with nothing short of sustained best efforts required for that accomplishment. This balance is exceedingly important.

How do we arrive at these annual Company objectives? How is a Company plan best created?

You go to your operating management, profit center managers or division managers. If your Company is a single unit operation, get out your last year's balance sheet and operating statement and start preparing "Company plan" work sheets based on the existing format.

Start with a performance picture in your mind that you feel will be difficult but possible to accomplish—all the basic management controls:

- Sales
- Gross Profit
- Operating Expenses
- Inventory Control
- Expense Control
- Net Operating Profit

In this chapter you will find a set of some thirty exhibits or forms that will help you in getting a "Company plan" or "Company objective" program started in your organization. Company objectives must be based on specific data supported by accurate detail as to source. A broad brush approach would be little more than guessing, and in this program guessing will not work. It is tedious but you must get to the exact sources of revenue and the detailed listing of expenses, investments and other factors, even to breaking down salary costs not only by expense category but by individual. Allowances must be made for salary adjustments and you may find it not only feasible but desirable to reduce personnel in some areas of operation, and increasing personnel in others where more productivity results.

With your Company objectives in mind you then set about outlining a program for accomplishment of those objectives. You have a target now. You want to make the best possible score and you get readings at monthly intervals.

Companies operating a number of "divisions" or "profit centers" follow this procedure in establishing annual Company objectives or a Company operating plan:

- distribute Company plan forms to each Division Manager
- require that all forms be completed and returned by a specified date well in advance of the close of the current fiscal year (3 months)
- when the completed forms are received from the Divisions, the Company Financial Officer reviews them and percentages are computed
- if a regional management structure exists, the Regional Manager reviews all company plan (by Division) figures submitted on Divisions operating within his region and makes notations as to recommended adjustments or changes
- the Executive Committee and Chief Executive Officer reviews each final set of division plan or objective figures submitted and makes any adjustment required to conform to overall Company objectives; final figures are approved by the Chief Executive Officer.

Here are sample work sheets used to submit proposed Company plan or profit plan figures. Reference is made first to the index page. Many of the forms listed do not have general or a broad application since the subject company is a large, diversified operation with a variety of profit centers in operation. Only elementary or essential forms are shown in this chapter. Those not having general application and/or use are omitted.

Schedule number designations are not important and may be ignored.

This is a system of Company plan forms that has been built from the ground up. It is working smoothly and effectively. The forms are illustrated simply to assist you and your associates in constructing your own set of "work sheets" based on your operating statement format. This material will help and it indicates the extent of detailed reporting required for a workable system.

The exercise is not unlike preparing a budget for your Company. You have done this. Go a step further and lock your budget into operational accomplishment, taking a monthly reading of progress in the process.

Following the index sheet, Figure 14-1, we have:

1. The Operating Statement, Figure 14-2
2. Sales, Returns, Allowances and Discounts, Figure 14-3
3. Sales and Cost of Goods Sold, Figure 14-4
4. Operating Expenses, Figures 14-5 through 14-5E
5. Payroll Compensation:
    a. delivery, Figure 14-6
    b. warehouse, Figure 14-6A
    c. salesman compensation, Figure 14-6B
    d. administrative sales, Figure 14-6C
    e. telephone order sales, Figure 14-6D
    f. data processing, Figure 14-6E

    g. management/executives, Figure 14-6F

    h. other administrative, Figure 14-6G

    i. buying, Figure 14-6H

    j. accounting, Figure 14-6I

    k. promotional monies paid, Figure 14-6J

6. Total Compensation and Payroll Taxes and Benefits, Figure 14-7

7. Employee Headcount by Classification, Figure 14-8

8. Contributions by Charitable Organizations, Figure 14-9

9. Subscriptions and Dues by Organizations, Figure 14-10

10. Maintenance and Repairs by Major Item, Figure 14-11

11. Consulting Fees by Individual/Company, Figure 14-12

12. Capital Expenditures—Purchase and/or Lease, Figures 14-13 and 14-13A

13. Other Revenue, Figure 14-14

The last nine items are presented on separate forms and itemized for special review because of the significant potential savings involved in these categories. You get results when you get specific.

COMPENSATION FOR ACCOMPLISHMENT

1. All Division Managers accomplishing division plan objectives receive a bonus stipulated in advance.

2. If as much as 80% of all divisions accomplish plan objectives, the regional management and staff people receive a stipulated bonus. Less than 80% accomplishment—no bonus.

BONUS

The total bonus package should amount to a reasonable percentage of Total Profit Increase realized as a result of the Company making its objectives or accomplishing plan.

RESULTS

Your interest in implementing the Company plan or Company objective program on an annual operating basis, with monthly reports, will be enhanced as you review the accomplishments reflected in the following reports. This is a record of actual accomplishment. Dollar figures have been omitted and only percentages are given to mask the relative size of each operation since these are existing businesses cooperating in providing material for this book. You will want to list dollar figures as well as percentages in your reports.

In this chapter we have presented two sets of forms as guides for use in implementing a workable management by objective program (the Company plan system). The first set of forms, Figures 14-1 through 14-14 are actually work papers to use in arriving at a Company plan. The second set of forms Figures 14-15 through 14-18, are monthly operating statements showing accomplishment to plan.

Remember, the fiscal year plan forms included in this chapter are, as stated, suggested forms only. You will note that they closely follow the monthly operating statement format

FISCAL YEAR PLAN

INDEX

SCHEDULE NUMBER	DESCRIPTION
1	OPERATING STATEMENT
2	SALES, RETURNS, ALLOWANCES, DISCOUNTS
2 - A	SALES & COST OF GOODS SOLD
3	OPERATING EXPENSES
3-A-1	PAYROLL COMPENSATION — DELIVERY
3-A-2	— WAREHOUSE
3-A-3	— SALESMEN COMPENSATION
3-A-4	— ADMINISTRATIVE SALES
3-A-5	— TELEPHONE ORDER SALES
3-A-6	— DATA PROCESSING (E.D.P.)
3-A-7	— MANAGEMENT / EXECUTIVES
3-A-8	— OTHER ADMINISTRATIVE
3-A-9	— BUYING
3-A-10	— ACCOUNTING
3-A-11	— PROMOTIONAL MONIES PAID

SCHEDULE NUMBER	DESCRIPTION
3 - B	TOTAL COMPENSATION AND PAYROLL TAXES AND BENEFITS
3 - C	EMPLOYEE HEADCOUNT BY CLASSIFICATION
3 - D	CONTRIBUTIONS BY CHARITABLE ORGANIZATIONS
3 - E	SUBSCRIPTIONS AND DUES BY ORGANIZATIONS
3 - F	MAINTENANCE AND REPAIRS BY MAJOR ITEMS
3 - G	CONSULTING FEES BY INDIVIDUAL / COMPANY
7	CAPITAL EXPENDITURE
8	OTHER REVENUE

Figure 14-1

163

FISCAL YEAR PLAN
OPERATING STATEMENT

($000.0)

SCHEDULE 1

SUB. 61 CENTER

DESCRIPTION	ACCT. NO.	SEP	OCT	NOV	DEC	JAN	FEB	MAR	APR	MAY	JUN	JUL	AUG	TOTAL F.Y. CUR.	EST. F.Y. PRIOR	9 MONTHS PRIOR YEAR
1. Gross Sales (Line 11 Sch. 2)																
2. Allowances (Line 14 Sch. 2)																
3. Returns (line 16 Sch. 2)																
4. Net Shipments (Line 1 - 2 + 3)																
5.																
6. Cost of Goods Sold																
7.																
8. Gross Margin (Line 4 - 6)																
9.																
10. Total Sales Discount (Line 25 Sch. 2)																
11.																
12. Gross Profit (Line 8 - 10)																
13.																
14. Total Operating Expenses (Sch. 3 Pg 6)																
15.																
16. Phase Expenses (Line 26 Sch. 8B)																
17. Phase Revenue (Line 10 Sch. 8A)																
18. Net Phase																
19.																
20. Net G.N.P. (Line 10 Sch. 8C)																
21.																
22. Net Microphase (Line 22 Sch. 8D)																
23.																
24. Other Revenue (Line 26 Sch 8)																
25.																
26. Income Before C.O.M. & Taxes																

Figure 14-2

FISCAL YEAR PLAN

SALES, RETURNS, ALLOWANCES, DISCOUNTS

($000)

SCHEDULE 2

SUB 61 CENTER

DESCRIPTION	ACCT. NO.	SEP	OCT	NOV	DEC	JAN	FEB	MAR	APR	MAY	JUN	JUL	AUG	TOTAL F.Y. CUR.	EST. F.Y.PRIOR	9 MONTHS PRIOR YEAR
1. Gross Sales Actual (+Estimate)																
2. Gross Sales (Trans to) Rec from other [DQ]																
3. Total (Line 1 plus 2)																
4.																
5. Working Days by Month Fiscal '76-'77																
6. Average Gross Sales/Day (Line 3÷5)																
7. Working Days by Month Fiscal '77-'78																
8. Adjusted '77-'78 Base (Line 6 X 7)																
9. % Increase Projected by Month																
10. $ Sales Increase projected (Line 8x9)																
11. Gross Sales Fiscal '78 (Line 8+10)																
12.																
13. Allowances - % per Month																
14. Allowances - $ (Line 11 X 13)	40401															
15. Returns - % per Month																
16. Returns - $(Line 11 X 15)	40402															
17. Total Allow + Returns (Line 14+16)																
18. Net Shipments (Line 11 - 17)																
19.																
20. Sales Discounts																
21. Discount % per month																
22. Discount $(Line 18 X 21)	40501															
23. Phase Allowance % per Month																
24. Phase Allowance $(Line 18 X 23)	40505															
25. Total Sales Discount (Line 22 + 24)																
26.																

Figure 14-3

FISCAL YEAR PLAN
SALES & COST OF GOODS SOLD
($000)

Schedule 2 - A

SUB 61   CENTER

DESCRIPTION	ACCT. NO.	SEP	OCT	NOV	DEC	JAN	FEB	MAR	APR	MAY	JUN	JUL	AUG	TOTAL F.Y. CUR.	EST. F.Y. PRIOR	9 MONTHS PRIOR YEAR
1. Gross Sales From Line 11 Sch. 2																
2.																
3. Regular %																
4. Regular $(Line 1 X 3)	40001															
5. Low Profit & Cost Plus %																
6. Low Profit + Cost Plus $(Line 1 X 5)	40002															
7. G. N. P. %																
8. G. N. P. $(Line 1 X 7)	40003															
9. Off-Line %																
10. Off-Line $(Line 1 X 9)	40004															
11.																
12.																
13. Cost of Goods Sold:																
14. Regular %																
15. Regular $(Line 4 X 14)	45101															
16. Low Profit + Cost Plus %																
17. Low Profit + Cost Plus $(Line 6X16)	45105															
18. G. N. P. 90%																
19. G. N. P. $(Line 8 X 18)	45106															
20. Off-Line %																
21. Off-Line $(Line 10 X 20)	45107															
22. Total COGS (Line 15+17+19+21)																
23. COGS Percent (Line 22 ÷ 1)																
24.																
25. Total Allow + Returns (Line 17 Sch 2)																
26. Cost on Allow + Returns (Line 23x25)	45117															

Figure 14-4

166

FISCAL YEAR PLAN
OPERATING EXPENSES

($000.0)

SUB. 61 CENTER _____

DESCRIPTION	ACCT. NO.	SEP	OCT	NOV	DEC	JAN	FEB	MAR	APR	MAY	JUN	JUL	AUG	TOTAL F.Y. CUR.	EST. F.Y. PRIOR	9 MONTHS PRIOR YEAR
1. Delivery Wages	70351															
2. Other Delivery Costs																
3. Outside Contract Delivery	76051															
4. Freight to Customers	77451															
5. Freight on Return to Mfgs.	77551															
6. Rental – Delivery Equipment	74451															
7. Fuel – Delivery Equipment	77351															
8. Repairs & Maint.-Delivery Equip.	75051															
9. Licenses & Permits – Del. Equip.	77251															
10. Other Delivery Expenses	79552															
11. Total Other Delivery Costs																
12.																
13. Salesmen Costs:																
14. Salary	60301															
15. Commission	60302															
16. Auto Rental	64401															
17. Total Salesmen Costs																
18.																
19. Warehouse Wages	70301															
20.																
21. Payroll Taxes & Benefits	91601															
22.																
23. Telephone	97901															
24. Utilities	98001															
25.																
26.																

Figure 14-5

167

FISCAL YEAR PLAN
OPERATING EXPENSES

($000.0)

SUB. 61 CENTER _____

DESCRIPTION	ACCT. NO.	SEP	OCT	NOV	DEC	JAN	FEB	MAR	APR	MAY	JUN	JUL	AUG	TOTAL F.Y. CUR.	EST. F.Y. PRIOR	9 MONTHS PRIOR YEAR
1. Administrative Sales Salaries	60201															
2. Telephone Order Sales Salaries	60401															
3. EDP Salaries	80301															
4. Administrative Salaries																
5. Management Salaries	90301															
6. Other Administrative Salaries	90401															
7. Buying Salaries	90402															
8. Accounting Dept. Salaries	90403															
9. Total Administrative Salaries																
10. Fixed Compensation																
11.																
12.																
13. Other Purchased Services																
14. Contract Jan. & Clean. Service	96301															
15. Plant Protection Service	96302															
16. Credit & Collection Fees	96401															
17. Legal Fees	96402															
18. Outside Warehousing Costs	79502															
19. Total Other Purchased Services																
20.																
21.																
22.																
23.																
24.																
25.																
26.																

Figure 14-5A

FISCAL YEAR PLAN
OPERATING EXPENSES

($000.0)

SUB. 61 CENTER

DESCRIPTION	ACCT. NO.	SEP	OCT	NOV	DEC	JAN	FEB	MAR	APR	MAY	JUN	JUL	AUG	TOTAL F.Y. CUR.	EST. F.Y. PRIOR	9 MONTHS PRIOR YEAR
1. Operating Supplies																
2. Selling Supplies	63101															
3. Packing & Shipping Supplies	73102															
4. Warehouse Supplies	73101															
5. Stationery & Office Supplies	93101															
6. Postage	93201															
7. Data Processing Supplies	83101															
8. Total Operating Supplies																
9.																
10.																
11. Travel & Entertainment																
12. Selling	62001															
13. Administrative	92001															
14. Total Travel & Entertainment																
15.																
16.																
17. Rentals																
18. Sales Automobiles	64402															
19. Occupancy	94001															
20. Office Equipment	94601															
21. Administrative Vehicles	94401															
22. EDP Equipment	84501															
23. Total Rentals																
24.																
25.																
26.																

Figure 14-5B

169

FISCAL YEAR PLAN
OPERATING EXPENSES

($000.0)

SUB. ___61___   CENTER ___

DESCRIPTION	ACCT. NO.	SEP	OCT	NOV	DEC	JAN	FEB	MAR	APR	MAY	JUN	JUL	AUG	TOTAL F.Y. CUR.	EST. F.Y. PRIOR	9 MONTHS PRIOR YEAR
1. Other Taxes																
2. Real Estate	97601															
3. Personal Property	97602															
4. Total Other Taxes																
5.																
6. Insurance																
7. Property	97701															
8. Self Insurance Losses	97801															
9. Total Insurance																
10.																
11. Repairs & Maintenance																
12. Building	75001															
13. Warehouse Equipment	75002															
14. Office Equipment	95001															
15. EDP Equipment	85001															
16. Total Repairs & Maintenance																
17.																
18. Depreciation																
19. Buildings	95103															
20. Leasehold Improvements	95104															
21. Machinery & Equipment	75101															
22. Office Furniture & Equipment	95101															
23. Total Depreciation																
24.																
25.																
26.																

Figure 14-5C

FISCAL YEAR PLAN
OPERATING EXPENSES

($000.0)

SUB. 61 CENTER

DESCRIPTION	ACCT. NO.	SEP	OCT	NOV	DEC	JAN	FEB	MAR	APR	MAY	JUN	JUL	AUG	TOTAL F.Y. CUR.	EST. F.Y. PRIOR	9 MONTHS PRIOR YEAR
1. Provision For Bad Debts	98101															
2.																
3. Other Expenses																
4. Other Selling	69501															
5. Other Occupancy	99301															
6. Other Warehouse	79501															
7. Business Licenses	97202															
8. Licenses & Permits-Adm.Vehicles	97203															
9. Donations	98201															
10. Subscriptions & Dues	98301															
11. Other Data Process. Expense	89501															
12. Other Administrative	99302															
13. Moving and Rearrangement Cost	99305															
14. Total Other Expenses																
15.																
16. Inter Department Charges																
17. Charges To Others *	99101															
18. Charges From Others	99201															
19. Total Inter Department Charges																
20.																
21.																
22.																
23. Promotional Monies Paid	60304															
24. Promotional Monies Received *	60305															
25. Net Promotional Monies																
26.																

* Brackets must be used for this line.

Figure 14-5D

171

FISCAL YEAR PLAN

OPERATING EXPENSE RECAP

($000.0)

	ACCT. NO.	SEP	OCT	NOV	DEC	JAN	FEB	MAR	APR	MAY	JUN	JUL	AUG	TOTAL F.Y. CUR.	EST. F.Y. PRIOR	9 MONTHS PRIOR YEAR
1. Delivery Wages																
2. Other Delivery Costs																
3. Salesmen Costs																
4. Warehouse Wages																
5. Payroll Taxes & Benefits																
6. Telephone & Telegraph																
7. Utilities																
8. Administrative Sales Salaries																
9. Telephone Order Sales Comp.																
10. EDP Salaries																
11. Administrative Salaries																
12. Other Purchased Services																
13. Operating Supplies																
14. Travel & Entertainment																
15. Rentals																
16. Other Taxes																
17. Insurance																
18. Repairs & Maintenance																
19. Depreciation																
20. Provision For Bad Debt																
21. Other Expenses																
22. Inter Department Charges																
23. Net Promotional Monies																
24.																
25.																
26. * Total Operating Expenses																

* (To Schedule 1 line 12)

Figure 14-5E

172

FISCAL YEAR PLAN
PAYROLL COMPENSATION

SCHEDULE 3 - A - 1

SUB. _____ CENTER _____

RATE _____

DELIVERY (TRUCK DRIVERS)

EMPLOYEE NAME	DUTIES	PRESENT PAYROLL	EST. AUG.	SEP	OCT	NOV	DEC	JAN	FEB	MAR	APR	MAY	JUN	JUL	AUG	TOTAL F.Y. CUR.
1.																
2.																
3.																
4.																
5.																
6.																
7.																
8.																
9.																
10.																
11.																
12.																
13.																
14.																
15.																
16.																
17.																
18.																
19. Total of Employee Rates																
20. Paid Hours																
21. Regular Payroll																
22. Overtime Rate																
23. Estimated Overtime Hours																
24. Overtime Payroll																
25. TOTAL PAYROLL																
26. TOTAL PEOPLE AT MONTH END																

* To Schedule 3 - B line 1   ** To Schedule 3 - C line 12

Figure 14-6

173

FISCAL YEAR PLAN
PAYROLL COMPENSATION

SCHEDULE 3 - A - 2

WAREHOUSE _____

RATE _____

SUB. _____ CENTER _____

EMPLOYEE NAME	DUTIES	PRESENT PAYROLL	EST. AUG.	SEP	OCT	NOV	DEC	JAN	FEB	MAR	APR	MAY	JUN	JUL	AUG	TOTAL F.Y. CUR.
1.																
2.																
3.																
4.																
5.																
6.																
7.																
8.																
9.																
10.																
11.																
12.																
13.																
14.																
15.																
16.																
17.																
18.																
19. Total of Employee Rates																
20. Paid Hours																
21. Regular Payroll																
22. Overtime Rate																
23. Estimated Overtime Hours																
24. Overtime Payroll																
25. TOTAL PAYROLL																
26. TOTAL PEOPLE AT MONTH END																

* To Schedule 3 - B line 3   ** To Schedule 3 - C line 5

* To Schedule 3 - B line 3

**

Figure 14-6A

174

FISCAL YEAR PLAN
PAYROLL COMPENSATION

SCHEDULE 3 - A - 3

SUB. _____ CENTER _____

SALESMEN COMPENSATION
DRAW/SALARY + COMMISSION (DOES NOT INCLUDE PM's)

RATE _____

EMPLOYEE NAME	DUTIES	PRESENT PAYROLL	EST. AUG.	SEP	OCT	NOV	DEC	JAN	FEB	MAR	APR	MAY	JUN	JUL	AUG	TOTAL F.Y. CUR.
1.																
2.																
3.																
4.																
5.																
6.																
7.																
8.																
9.																
10.																
11.																
12.																
13.																
14.																
15.																
16.																
17.																
18.																
19. Total of Employee Rates																
20. Paid Hours																
21. Regular Payroll																
22. Overtime Rate																
23. Estimated Overtime Hours																
24. Overtime Payroll																
25. TOTAL PAYROLL																
26. TOTAL PEOPLE AT MONTH END																

* To Schedule 3 - B line 2   ** To Schedule 3 - C line 2

* To Schedule 3 - B line 2

** To Schedule 3 - C line 2

175

Figure 14-6B

FISCAL YEAR PLAN
PAYROLL COMPENSATION

SCHEDULE 3 - A - 4 ___

SUB. ___ CENTER ___

RATE ___

ADMINISTRATIVE SALES SALARIES

EMPLOYEE NAME	DUTIES	PRESENT PAYROLL	EST. AUG.	SEP	OCT	NOV	DEC	JAN	FEB	MAR	APR	MAY	JUN	JUL	AUG	TOTAL F.Y. CUR.
1.																
2.																
3.																
4.																
5.																
6.																
7.																
8.																
9.																
10.																
11.																
12.																
13.																
14.																
15.																
16.																
17.																
18.																
19. Total of Employee Rates																
20. Paid Hours																
21. Regular Payroll																
22. Overtime Rate																
23. Estimated Overtime Hours																
24. Overtime Payroll																
25. TOTAL PAYROLL																
26. TOTAL PEOPLE AT MONTH END																

* To Schedule 3 - B line 4   ** To Schedule 3 - C line 1

*

**

Figure 14-6C

176

FISCAL YEAR PLAN
PAYROLL COMPENSATION

TELEPHONE ORDER SALES

SCHEDULE 3 - A - _5_

SUB. _____ CENTER _____

RATE _____

EMPLOYEE NAME / DUTIES	PRESENT PAYROLL	EST. AUG.	SEP	OCT	NOV	DEC	JAN	FEB	MAR	APR	MAY	JUN	JUL	AUG	TOTAL F.Y. CUR.
1.															
2.															
3.															
4.															
5.															
6.															
7.															
8.															
9.															
10.															
11.															
12.															
13.															
14.															
15.															
16.															
17.															
18.															
19. Total of Employee Rates															
20. Paid Hours															
21. Regular Payroll															
22. Overtime Rate															
23. Estimated Overtime Hours															
24. Overtime Payroll															
25. TOTAL PAYROLL															
26. TOTAL PEOPLE AT MONTH END															

* To Schedule 3 - B line 5   ** To Schedule 3 - C line 3

* To Schedule 3 - B line 3

** To Schedule 3 - C line 3

Figure 14-6D

177

DATA PROCESSING (E.D.P.)

FISCAL YEAR PLAN
PAYROLL COMPENSATION

RATE _____

SCHEDULE 3 - A - 6

SUB. _____ CENTER _____

EMPLOYEE NAME	DUTIES	PRESENT PAYROLL	EST. AUG.	SEP	OCT	NOV	DEC	JAN	FEB	MAR	APR	MAY	JUN	JUL	AUG	TOTAL F.Y. CUR.
1.																
2.																
3.																
4.																
5.																
6.																
7.																
8.																
9.																
10.																
11.																
12.																
13.																
14.																
15.																
16.																
17.																
18.																
19. Total of Employee Rates																
20. Paid Hours																
21. Regular Payroll																
22. Overtime Rate																
23. Estimated Overtime Hours																
24. Overtime Payroll																
25. TOTAL PAYROLL																
26. TOTAL PEOPLE AT MONTH END																

* To Schedule 3 - B line 6   ** To Schedule 3 - C line 6

* To Schedule 3 - B line 6

** To Schedule 3 - C line 6

Figure 14-6E

178

FISCAL YEAR PLAN
PAYROLL COMPENSATION

SCHEDULE 3 - A - 7 ____

RATE ____

SUB. ____ CENTER ____

MANAGEMENT/EXECUTIVES

EMPLOYEE NAME	DUTIES	PRESENT PAYROLL	EST. AUG.	SEP	OCT	NOV	DEC	JAN	FEB	MAR	APR	MAY	JUN	JUL	AUG	TOTAL F.Y. CUR.
1.																
2.																
3.																
4.																
5.																
6.																
7.																
8.																
9.																
10.																
11.																
12.																
13.																
14.																
15.																
16.																
17.																
18.																
19. Total of Employee Rates																
20. Paid Hours																
21. Regular Payroll																
22. Overtime Rate																
23. Estimated Overtime Hours																
24. Overtime Payroll																
25. TOTAL PAYROLL																
26. TOTAL PEOPLE AT MONTH END																

* To Schedule 3 - B line 7   ** To Schedule 3 - C line 7

*
**

Figure 14-6F

FISCAL YEAR PLAN
PAYROLL COMPENSATION

SCHEDULE 3 - A - 8
SUB. _____ CENTER _____
RATE _____

OTHER ADMINISTRATIVE

EMPLOYEE NAME	DUTIES	PRESENT PAYROLL	EST. AUG.	SEP	OCT	NOV	DEC	JAN	FEB	MAR	APR	MAY	JUN	JUL	AUG	TOTAL F.Y. CUR.
1.																
2.																
3.																
4.																
5.																
6.																
7.																
8.																
9.																
10.																
11.																
12.																
13.																
14.																
15.																
16.																
17.																
18.																
19. Total of Employee Rates																
20. Paid Hours																
21. Regular Payroll																
22. Overtime Rate																
23. Estimated Overtime Hours																
24. Overtime Payroll																
25. TOTAL PAYROLL																
26. TOTAL PEOPLE AT MONTH END																

* To Schedule 3 - B line 8   ** To Schedule 3 - C line 8

*
**

Figure 14-6G

180

FISCAL YEAR PLAN
PAYROLL COMPENSATION

BUYING

SCHEDULE 3 - A - 9

SUB. _____ CENTER

RATE _____

EMPLOYEE NAME	DUTIES	PRESENT PAYROLL	EST. AUG.	SEP	OCT	NOV	DEC	JAN	FEB	MAR	APR	MAY	JUN	JUL	AUG	TOTAL F.Y. CUR.
1.																
2.																
3.																
4.																
5.																
6.																
7.																
8.																
9.																
10.																
11.																
12.																
13.																
14.																
15.																
16.																
17.																
18.																
19. Total of Employee Rates																
20. Paid Hours																
21. Regular Payroll																
22. Overtime Rate																
23. Estimated Overtime Hours																
24. Overtime Payroll																
25. TOTAL PAYROLL																
26. TOTAL PEOPLE AT MONTH END																

* To Schedule 3 - B line 9   ** To Schedule 3 - C line 9

181

Figure 14-6H

FISCAL YEAR PLAN
PAYROLL COMPENSATION

SCHEDULE 3 - A - 10

SUB. _____ CENTER _____

ACCOUNTING

RATE _____

EMPLOYEE NAME	DUTIES	PRESENT PAYROLL	EST. AUG.	SEP	OCT	NOV	DEC	JAN	FEB	MAR	APR	MAY	JUN	JUL	AUG	TOTAL F.Y. CUR.
1.																
2.																
3.																
4.																
5.																
6.																
7.																
8.																
9.																
10.																
11.																
12.																
13.																
14.																
15.																
16.																
17.																
18.																
19. Total of Employee Rates																
20. Paid Hours																
21. Regular Payroll																
22. Overtime Rate																
23. Estimated Overtime Hours																
24. Overtime Payroll																
25. TOTAL PAYROLL																
26. TOTAL PEOPLE AT MONTH END																

* To Schedule 3 - B line 10   ** To Schedule 3 - C line 10

*

**

Figure 14-6I

182

FISCAL YEAR PLAN
PAYROLL COMPENSATION

SCHEDULE 3 - A - 11

SUB. _____ CENTER _____

PROMOTIONAL MONIES PAID _____

RATE _____

EMPLOYEE NAME	DUTIES	PRESENT PAYROLL	EST. AUG.	SEP	OCT	NOV	DEC	JAN	FEB	MAR	APR	MAY	JUN	JUL	AUG	TOTAL F.Y. CUR.
1.																
2.																
3.																
4.																
5.																
6.																
7.																
8.																
9.																
10.																
11.																
12.																
13.																
14.																
15.																
16.																
17.																
18.																
19. Total of Employee Rates																
20. Paid Hours																
21. Regular Payroll																
22. Overtime Rate																
23. Estimated Overtime Hours																
24. Overtime Payroll																
25. TOTAL PAYROLL																
26. TOTAL PEOPLE AT MONTH END																

* To Schedule 3 - B line 11

Figure 14-6J

FISCAL YEAR PLAN
TOTAL COMPENSATION AND PAYROLL TAXES

SCHEDULE 3 B

SUB. _____ CENTER

DESCRIPTION	SEP	OCT	NOV	DEC	JAN	FEB	MAR	APR	MAY	JUN	JUL	AUG	TOTAL F.Y. CUR.	EST F.Y. PRIOR
1. Delivery Wages														
2. Salesmen Compensation														
3. Warehouse Wages														
4. Administrative Sales Salaries														
5. Telephone Order Sales														
6. Data Processing Salaries (E.D.P.)														
7. Management/Executive														
8. Other Administrative Salaries														
9. Buying Salaries														
10. Accounting Salaries														
11. Promotional Monies Paid														
12. Total Compensation (Lines 1-11)														
13. Payroll Taxes & Benefits 17%x Line 12														

Post Lines 1-13 to Respective Line on Schedule 3

Figure 14-7

184

FISCAL YEAR PLAN

EMPLOYEE HEADCOUNT BY CLASSIFICATION

SCHEDULE 3-C

SUB. _____ CENTER _____

DESCRIPTION	EST AUG	SEP	OCT	NOV	DEC	JAN	FEB	MAR	APR	MAY	JUN	JUL	AUG	F.Y. CUR.	F.Y. PRIOR
1. Administrative Sales															
2. Salesmen															
3. Telephone Order Sales															
4. Total Sales Personnel															
5. Warehouse															
6. Data Processing (E.D.P.)															
7. Management/Executive															
8. Other Administrative															
9. Buying															
10. Accounting															
11. Total Excluding Drivers															
12. Delivery (Truck Drivers)															
13. Total Employees															

Figure 14-8

185

FISCAL YEAR PLAN

CONTRIBUTIONS BY CHARITABLE ORGANIZATION

($000.0)

SCHEDULE 3-D

SUB._____ CENTER _____

DESCRIPTION	ACCT. NO.	SEP	OCT	NOV	DEC	JAN	FEB	MAR	APR	MAY	JUN	JUL	AUG	TOTAL F.Y. CUR.	EST. F.Y. PRIOR	9 MONTHS PRIOR YEAR
1.	98201															
2.																
3.																
4.																
5.																
6.																
7.																
8.																
9.																
10.																
11.																
12.																
13.																
14.																
15.																
16.																
17.																
18.																
19.																
20.																
21.																
22.																
23.																
24.																
25.																
26. Total Contributions (To Schedule 3)	98201															

Figure 14-9

FISCAL YEAR PLAN

SUBSCRIPTIONS & DUES BY ORGANIZATION

SUB._____ CENTER_____

($000.0)

DESCRIPTION	ACCT. NO.	SEP	OCT	NOV	DEC	JAN	FEB	MAR	APR	MAY	JUN	JUL	AUG	TOTAL F.Y. CUR.	EST. F.Y. PRIOR	9 MONTHS PRIOR YEAR
1.	98301															
2.																
3.																
4.																
5.																
6.																
7.																
8.																
9.																
10.																
11.																
12.																
13.																
14.																
15.																
16.																
17.																
18.																
19.																
20.																
21.																
22.																
23.																
24.																
25. Total Subscriptions & Dues	98301															
26.																

(To Schedule 3)

Figure 14-10

187

FISCAL YEAR PLAN
MAINTENANCE & REPAIRS BY MAJOR ITEM
($000.0)

SCHEDULE 3-F

SUB. _____ CENTER _____

DESCRIPTION	ACCT. NO.	SEP	OCT	NOV	DEC	JAN	FEB	MAR	APR	MAY	JUN	JUL	AUG	TOTAL F.Y. CUR.	EST. F.Y. PRIOR	9 MONTHS PRIOR YEAR
1.																
2.																
3.																
4.																
5.																
6.																
7.																
8.																
9.																
10.																
11.																
12.																
13.																
14.																
15.																
16.																
17.																
18.																
19.																
20.																
21.																
22.																
23.																
24.																
25.																
26. Total Maintenance & Repairs																

(To Schedule 3)

Figure 14-11

188

FISCAL YEAR PLAN
CONSULTING FEES BY INDIVIDUAL/COMPANY

($000.0)

SUB._____ CENTER_____

DESCRIPTION	ACCT. NO.	SEP	OCT	NOV	DEC	JAN	FEB	MAR	APR	MAY	JUN	JUL	AUG	TOTAL F.Y. CUR.	EST. F.Y. PRIOR	9 MONTHS PRIOR YEAR
1.	96101															
2.																
3.																
4.																
5.																
6.																
7.																
8.																
9.																
10.																
11.																
12.																
13.																
14.																
15.																
16.																
17.																
18.																
19.																
20.																
21.																
22.																
23.																
24.																
25.																
26. Total Consulting Fees	96101															

(To Schedule 3)

Figure 14-12

189

FISCAL YEAR PLAN

CAPITAL EXPENDITURES – PURCHASE

($000.0)

SUB._____ CENTER _____

PROJECT DESCRIPTION	INVEST- MENT CATE- GORY *	TOTAL APPROP. **	MONTH OF EXPENDITURE												F.Y. CUR.	CARRY- OVER APPROP.
			SEP	OCT	NOV	DEC	JAN	FEB	MAR	APR	MAY	JUN	JUL	AUG		
1.																
2.																
3.																
4.																
5.																
6.																
7.																
8.																
9.																
10.																
11.																
12.																
13.																
14.																
15.																
16.																
17.																
18.																
19.																
20.																
21.																
22.																
23.																
24.																
25.																
26.																
27.																
28.																
29.																
30.																
31.																
32. Grand Total																

* Investment Category: 1 – Profit-Adding   2 – Profit-Maintaining   3 – Replacement   4 – Other

** Indicate amounts carried over from prior year.

NOTE: Attach supplemental schedule indicating rate of return and payback for projects over $10,000.

Figure 14-13

FISCAL YEAR PLAN
CAPITAL EXPENDITURES - LEASE

($000.0)

SUB. _____
CENTER _____

| PROJECT DESCRIPTION | INVEST-MENT CATE-GORY* | TOTAL COMMIT-MENT | MONTH OF EXPENDITURE | | | | | | | | | | | | LEASE EXPENSE F.Y. CUR. | REMAINING COMMIT-MENT |
			SEP	OCT	NOV	DEC	JAN	FEB	MAR	APR	MAY	JUN	JUL	AUG		
1.																
2.																
3.																
4.																
5.																
6.																
7.																
8.																
9.																
10.																
11.																
12.																
13.																
14.																
15.																
16.																
17.																
18.																
19.																
20.																
21.																
22.																
23.																
24.																
25.																
26.																
27.																
28.																
29.																
30.																
31.																
32. Grand Total																

* Investment Category: 1 – Profit-Adding   2 – Profit-Maintaining   3 – Replacement   4 – Other
NOTE: Attach supplemental schedule indicating rate of return and payback for projects over $10,000.

Figure 14-13A

FISCAL YEAR PLAN

OTHER REVENUE

($000.0)

SCHEDULE 8

SUB 61 CENTER

DESCRIPTION	ACCT. NO.	SEP	OCT	NOV	DEC	JAN	FEB	MAR	APR	MAY	JUN	JUL	AUG	TOTAL F.Y. CUR.	EST. F.Y. PRIOR	9 MONTHS PRIOR YEAR
1. Interest on Receivables	44001															
2.																
3. Miscellaneous Other Income	44304															
4.																
5. Fees and Commissions	44301															
6.																
7. Interest or Finance Charges	42401															
8.																
9. Rental Income	43001															
10.																
11.																
12.																
13.																
14.																
15.																
16.																
17.																
18.																
19.																
20.																
21.																
22.																
23.																
24.																
25.																
26. Total Other Revenue																

Figure 14-14

192

FISCAL YEAR END
Issued (Date)

	CURRENT MONTH			YEAR TO DATE		
	Actual Current Year %	Actual Prior Year %	Profit Plan %	Actual Current Year %	Actual Prior Year %	Profit Plan %
Gross Sales	10.0	10.8	10.8	11.0	11.6	11.6
Allowances	.1-	.0	.0	.2-	.0	.0
Returns	1.2-	1.3-	2.1-	1.9-	1.9-	2.1-
Net Shipments	100.0	100.0	100.0	100.0	100.0	100.0
Cost of Goods Sold	82.9	82.8	81.7	82.6	81.7	81.7
Inventory Adjustments	1.0-	4.0-	.0	.0	.3-	.0
Gross Margin	18.2	21.3	18.3	17.5	18.6	18.3
Less Sales Discounts	7.1-	7.9-	7.4-	7. -	7.4-	7.4-
Gross Profit	11.1	13.4	10.8	10.2	11.2	10.8
Operating Expenses						
Delivery Wages	.6	.6	.7	.6	.7	.7
Other Delivery Costs	.3	.3	.3	.2	.3	.3
Total Delivery Costs	1.0	.8	.9	.8	.9	.9
Salesmens Costs	.8	.8	.7	.8	.8	.8
Warehouse Wages	1.2	1.3	1.4	1.	1.5	1.5
Payroll Taxes & Benefits	.4	.7	.4	.5	.5	.4
Telephone	.2	.2	.2	.2	.2	.2
Utilities	.1	.1	.1	.1	.1	.1
Admin. & Other Sales Comp.	.1	.1	.1	.1	.1	.1
Telephone Order Sales Comp.	.2	.3	.3	.3	.3	.3
EDP Salaries	.2	.2	.2	.	.2	.2
Administrative Salaries	.3	.3	.3	.3	.3	.3
Fixed Compensation	.8	.9	.9	.9	1.0	.9
Other Purchased Services	.0	.0	.0	.	.0	.0
Operating Supplies	.2	.2	.1	.2	.2	.1
Travel and Entertainment	.0	.0	.0	.0	.0	.0
Rentals	.3	.3	.3	.	.3	.3
Taxes and Insurance	.2	.2	.2	.2	.2	.2
Advertising & Sales Prom.	.0	.0	.0	.0	.0	.0
Repairs and Maintenance	.1	.0	.0	.1	.0	.0
Depreciation	.2	.1	.0	.	.1	.0
Provision for Bad Debts	.0	.0	.0	.0	.0	.0
Other Expenses	.0	.0	.0	.0	.0	.0
Net Promotional Monies	.0	.0	.0	.0	.0	.0
Total Operating Expenses	5.4	5.5	5.3	5.3	5.6	5.3
R & D Items						
Item No. 1	.0	.0	.0	.0	.0	.0
Item No. 2	.0	.0	.0	.	.0	.0
Item No. 3	1.5	.2	.3	.4	.3	.3
Item No. 4	.4	.3	.3	.4	.3	.3
Item No. 5	1.0-	.1	.0	.0	.0	.0
Other Revenue	.0	.0	.0	.0	.0	.0
Income Before C.O.M. (Taxes)	4.6	8.0	5.6	4.8	5.6	5.6
Cost of Money Charge	.9	.8	.9	.	.9	.9
Income Before Taxes	3.7	7.2	4.7	4.0	4.7	4.7
RETURN ON INVESTMENT	52.1	109.6	63.2	54.5	63.4	62.1

Figure 14-15

SUBJECT COMPANY "B"
COMPARATIVE INCOME STATEMENT

FISCAL YEAR END
Issued (Date)

	CURRENT MONTH			YEAR TO DATE		
	Actual Current Year %	Actual Prior Year %	Profit Plan %	Actual Current Year %	Actual Prior Year %	Profit Plan %
Gross Sales	110.7	109.6	96.4	99.9	93.1	90.0
Allowances	.8-	.0	.0	.7-	.0	.0
Returns	2.8-	.1-	2.7-	3. -	2.4-	2.7-
Net Shipments	100.0	100.0	100.0	100.0	100.0	100.0
Cost of Goods Sold	83.0	83.5	80.9	82.1	81.3	80.9
Inventory Adjustments	5.8-	3.7-	.0	.5-	.3-	.0
Gross Margin	22.9	20.3	19.1	18.	19.1	19.1
Less Sales Discounts	7.8-	7.1-	8.3-	7.9-	8.0-	8.3-
Gross Profit	15.0	13.1	10.7	10.4	11.0	10.7
Operating Expenses						
Delivery Wages	.7	.6	.7	.7	.7	.7
Other Delivery Costs	.3	.2	.3	.3	.2	.3
Total Delivery Costs	1.0	.8	1.0	1.0	1.0	1.0
Salesmens Costs	.8	.8	.8	.	.8	.8
Warehouse Wages	1.1	1.0	1.3	1.3	1.3	1.3
Payroll Taxes & Benefits	.4	.6	.4	.5	.5	.4
Telephone	.2	.1	.2	.	.2	.2
Utilities	.1	.1	.1	.1	.1	.1
Admin. & Other Sales Comp.	.1	.1	.1	.1	.1	.1
Telephone Order Sales Comp.	.2	.2	.2	.2	.2	.2
EDP Salaries	.2	.1	.2	.2	.2	.2
Administrative Salaries	.3	.3	.3	.3	.4	.3
Fixed Compensation	.7	.7	.9	.8	.9	.9
Other Purchased Services	.0	.0	.1	.	.1	.1
Operating Supplies	.0	.3	.1	.1	.2	.2
Travel and Entertainment	.0	.0	.0	.0	.0	.0
Rentals	.3	.3	.3	.	.4	.4
Taxes and Insurance	.3	.2	.2	.3	.3	.3
Advertising & Sales Prom.	.0	.0	.0	.0	.0	.0
Repairs and Maintenance	.1	.1	.1	.1	.1	.1
Depreciation	.0	.1	.1	.	.1	.1
Provision for Bad Debts	.0	.2	.0	.0	.0	.0
Other Expenses	.1	.0	.1	.1	.1	.1
Net Promotional Monies	.0	.0	.0	.0	.0	.0
Total Operating Expenses	5.0	5.2	5.4	5.6	5.8	5.7
R & D Items						
Item No. 1	.0	.0	.0	.0	.0	.0
Item No. 2	.1	.0	.0	.	.0	.0
Item No. 3	1.5	.2	.3	.5	.3	.3
Item No. 4	.5	.3	.3	.4	.3	.3
Item No. 5	.9-	.1	.0	.0	.0	.0
Other Revenue	.0	.0	.0	.0	.1	.0
Income Before C.O.M. (Taxes)	9.0	8.0	5.4	4.8	5.3	5.1
Cost of Money Charge	.8	.7	.8	.9	1.1	1.0
Income Before Taxes	8.2	7.3	4.5	3.7	4.3	4.1
RETURN ON INVESTMENT	123.4	128.3	64.6	48.6	48.5	49.0

Figure 14-16

SUBJECT COMPANY "C"
COMPARATIVE INCOME STATEMENT

FISCAL YEAR END
Issued (Date)

	CURRENT MONTH						YEAR TO DATE					
	Actual Current Year	%	Actual Prior Year	%	Profit Plan	%	Actual Current Year	%	Actual Prior Year	%	Profit Plan	%
Gross Sales	97.9		79.2		97.4		98.9		94.5		97.1	
Allowances	.6-		.0		.0		.8-		.0		.0	
Returns	1.8-		1.8-		2.5-		2.5-		2.3-		2.5-	
Net Shipments	100.0		100.0		100.0		100.0		100.0		100.0	
Cost of Goods Sold	82.5		82.2		80.9		81.9		80.9		80.9	
Inventory Adjustments	4.8-		5.4-		.0		.4-		.4-		.0	
Gross Margin	22.3		23.3		19.1		18.6		19.6		19.1	
Less Sales Discounts	7.8-		8.0-		8.1-		7.9-		7.8-		8.1-	
Gross Profit	14.5		15.2		10.9		10.6		11.7		10.9	
Operating Expenses												
Delivery Wages	.6		.6		.8		.7		.8		.9	
Other Delivery Costs	.3		.3		.2		.3		.3		.3	
Total Delivery Costs	.9		.9		1.1		1.0		1.0		1.1	
Salesmens Costs	.9		.9		.9		.9		.9		.9	
Warehouse Wages	1.2		1.7		1.4		1.4		1.8		1.5	
Payroll Taxes & Benefits	.4		.9		.5		.5		.5		.5	
Telephone	.2		.2		.2		.2		.2		.2	
Utilities	.1		.1		.1		.1		.1		.1	
Admin. & Other Sales Comp.	.0		.1		.1		.1		.1		.1	
Telephone Order Sales Comp.	.2		.3		.3		.2		.3		.3	
EDP Salaries	.2		.2		.2		.		.2		.2	
Administrative Salaries	.3		.3		.3		.3		.4		.4	
Fixed Compensation	.8		.9		.9		.9		1.1		.9	
Other Purchased Services	.0		.0		.0		.		.0		.0	
Operating Supplies	.4		.3		.2		.2		.2		.2	
Travel and Entertainment	.0		.1		.0		.0		.0		.0	
Rentals	.3		.3		.4		.0		.0		.0	
Taxes and Insurance	.2		.2		.2		.		.4		.4	
Advertising & Sales Prom.	.0		.0		.0		.2		.2		.2	
Repairs and Maintenance	.1		.1		.1		.0		.0		.0	
Depreciation	.3		.1		.1		.1		.1		.1	
Provision for Bad Debts	.0		.7		.1		.1		.1		.1	
Other Expenses	.0		.1		.0		.1		.2		.0	
Net Promotional Monies	.0		.0		.1-		.0		.0		.1-	
Total Operating Expenses	5.7		7.4		5.8		6.1		6.8		6.0	
R & D Items												
Item No. 1	.0		.0		.0		.0		.0		.0	
Item No. 2	.0		.0		.0		.		.0		.0	
Item No. 3	1.9		.4		.3		.6		.4		.3	
Item No. 4	.5		.3		.3		.4		.3		.3	
Item No. 5	1.2-		.0		.0		.1-		.0		.0	
Other Revenue	.1		.0		.0		.1		.1		.1	
Income Before C.O.M. (Taxes)	7.6		7.6		5.2		4.5		4.9		5.0	
Cost of Money Charge	.9		.9		.9		1.		1.0		1.0	
Income Before Taxes	6.7		6.7		4.4		3.6		3.9		4.0	
RETURN ON INVESTMENT	92.3		85.5		61.5		44.8		45.9		49.1	

Figure 14-17

195

	CURRENT MONTH			YEAR TO DATE		
	Actual Current Year / %	Actual Prior Year / %	Profit Plan / %	Actual Current Year / %	Actual Prior Year / %	Profit Plan / %
Gross Sales	60.8	71.1	69.0	61.7	62.7	64.1
Allowances	.2-	.0	.0	.5-	.0	.0
Returns	1.6-	.0	2.4-	2. -	2.2-	2.4-
Net Shipments	100.0	100.0	100.0	100.0	100.0	100.0
Cost of Goods Sold	83.0	83.0	81.0	81.7	81.4	81.0
Inventory Adjustments	7.7-	8.6-	.0	.7-	.9-	.0
Gross Margin	24.8	25.8	19.0	19.	19.5	19.0
Less Sales Discounts	6.2-	7.2-	7.7-	7.4-	7.4-	7.7-
Gross Profit	18.5	18.5	11.2	11.6	12.0	11.2
Operating Expenses						
Delivery Wages	.4	.3	.4	.4	.4	.4
Other Delivery Costs	.7	.8	.7	.9	1.0	.9
Total Delivery Costs	1.1	1.1	1.1	1.3	1.4	1.3
Salesmens Costs	.7	.8	.8	.8	.9	.8
Warehouse Wages	1.4	1.3	1.4	1.6	1.7	1.5
Payroll Taxes & Benefits	.4	.7	.4	.5	.5	.4
Telephone	.3	.4	.4	.	.5	.4
Utilities	.1	.1	.1	.1	.1	.1
Admin. & Other Sales Comp.	.1	.1	.1	.2	.2	.2
Telephone Order Sales Comp.	.3	.2	.2	.2	.3	.2
EDP Salaries	.3	.2	.2	.3	.3	.3
Administrative Salaries	.5	.5	.5	.5	.6	.6
Fixed Compensation	1.1	1.1	1.1	1.4 — ?	1.4	1.2
Other Purchased Services	.0	.0	.0	.1	.1	.0
Operating Supplies	.1	.1	.2	.2	.2	.2
Travel and Entertainment	.1	.0	.0	.	.1	.0
Rentals	.5	.5	.5	.6	.6	.6
Taxes and Insurance	.3	.3	.3	.3	.4	.3
Advertising & Sales Prom.	.0	.0	.0	.	.0	.0
Repairs and Maintenance	.1	.1	.0	.0	.0	.0
Depreciation	.1	.1	.1	.	.1	.1
Provision for Bad Debts	.1	.2-	.1	.1	.0	.1
Other Expenses	.0	.0	.0	.0	.0	.0
Net Promotional Monies	.0	.0	.0	.0	.0	.0
Total Operating Expenses	6.5	6.2	6.4	7.4	8.0	7.1
R & D Items						
Item No. 1	.0	.0	.0	.0	.0	.0
Item No. 2	.0	.0	.0	.	.0	.0
Item No. 3	1.6	.6	.4	.7	.5	.4
Item No. 4	.5	.5	.5	.6	.5	.5
Item No. 5	1.0-	.0	.1	.0	.0	.0
Other Revenue	.0	.0	.0	.0	.0	.0
Income Before C.O.M. (Taxes)	11.0	12.2	5.0	4.1	4.1	4.2
Cost of Money Charge	1.0	.8	.8	1.1	1.0	1.0
Income Before Taxes	10.0	11.3	4.2	3.1	3.0	3.2
RETURN ON INVESTMENT	118.4	162.9	62.8	34.0	34.8	40.3

Figure 14-18

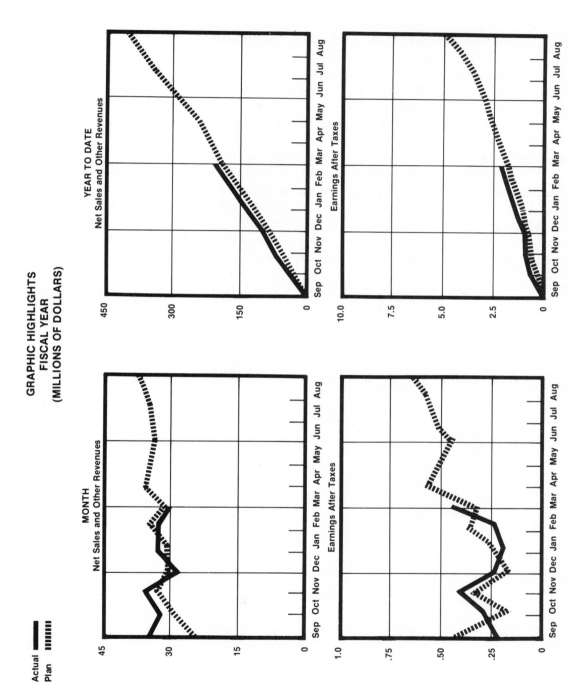

Figure 14-19

197

with appropriate subheadings and a logical sequence of income and operation expense accounts. It is suggested that, using your own monthly operating statement forms, you prepare your own Company plan or Company objective forms. This will greatly simplify submitting Company plan figures as well as using the "monthly" and "year to date" reporting procedure since all that is necessary is to simply "plug in" the Company plan figures for comparison with the actual "current month" and "year to date" figures as well as the "same month last year" and "year to date prior year." In this way you will have a logical and easily implemented reporting format for your particular company.

The forms used in reporting results are simply reproductions of monthly operating statements with dollar figures omitted and percentages only shown.

You will note, in Figure 14-19, that those companies tending to underestimate sales in Company plan figures generally experienced the highest return on investment when sales exceeded expectations or plan. Company investment and expenses generally have been held at lower levels. This is an indication that *increased investment requirements do not necessarily follow the sales trend if real incentives exist to control company investments in inventories, receivables and other controllable areas of capital investment.*

15

THE PERCEPTIVE DIRECTOR

Directors who listen and do their homework are needed by top management; combativeness is not strength; attacking problems, not people, in quest of solutions; positive helpfulness.

THE CHALLENGE

The corporate director plays an important and necessary role. Elected, as a rule, by shareholders at their annual meeting, he serves on a board presided over by a chairman who, in many cases, is also the company's chief executive officer.

A director must be informed. He must probe tactfully into company problems in a constructive way, but his role is not that of a critic of the chief executive officer.

A director who views his responsibility to shareholders as one in which he criticizes adversely and sometimes challenges management decisions, on an "after the fact" basis, is a disruptive force. Such a director renders a disservice to the shareholders he represents.

A good director is a good listener who has done his homework well in advance of each meeting. He has, for example, located and put his finger on the essence of some company problem and wants to know more about it.

- How the company got into the difficult situation?
- What steps are being taken to remedy the problem?
- What is the timetable for improvement?

One of the most able and constructive directors I have observed in action consistently followed this procedure:

- First, he tried to put himself in the place of chief executive officer to see the problem from his point of view. And, he usually succeeded.
- He listened attentively and without interruption to what the chairman was saying.
- In trying to understand the chairman's position, he was not inwardly contentious.
- He listened to *how* everything was said.
- He even listened to *what was not said*.

This concentration enabled full, uninterrupted communication to take place. After listening carefully and having the problem clearly defined in his mind, his response and handling of problems invariably consisted of a series of tactful, soft spoken questions, with notes being made on a memorandum pad as responses were given.

I have known this procedure to continue for a protracted period of time, always followed by an apology to the Board for the time consumed. Generally there was never a single declarative sentence regarding the problem being probed. And, the same low questioning voice was never once raised above a quiet tone of interested and helpful inquiry.

The formula:

1. How did we get into this problem?
2. What specific steps are being taken to get us out?
3. Do you think they will work?
4. What is the timetable for improvement?

Now, shall we work to that end, and we will check out the results at our next meeting—O.K.?

On the board of directors, it is not the critic that counts; not the man who points out how the chief executive officer may have stumbled and erred in judgment or as a doer of deeds, or how he may have done better.

The chief executive officer is in the heat of a continuing day-to-day competitive battle. He rarely has the luxury of length of time for reflection and quiet, unhurried consideration of all factors involved in making operating decisions that must be made at the time—decisions that often have far-reaching effects on his company. He is, and must be, essentially a man of action. As an honest and able man, he needs and deserves the constructive support of every member of the board of directors.

The director does enjoy the luxury of time in studying and evaluating decisions made—90 days of time between quarterly meetings. Keep that fact in mind and your service on any board will be more effective for the company and more rewarding for you.

It seems almost elementary to speak of the need for a director to listen but how many of you have served on boards where a number of side conversations between directors were in progress when the Chairman was providing important informative facts not accompanied by written memoranda for later immediate reference?

One conversation at a time is essential to a productive board meeting. No one can listen to two conversations at the same time and understand the content of either one of them.

Avoid distractions of every kind such as rummaging through papers in your briefcase. Share the responsibility for communication. Don't waste the advantage of thought speed. Most of us think at the rate of 500 words a minute but we are capable of talking at the rate of only 125 words per minute. Don't waste the 4:1 ratio in your favor as a listener by not concentrating on the speaker. Avoid distracting thoughts or ever trying to think ahead of the speaker. Stay with him and you will be surprised at how much of the input you are able to retain. This is one of the reasons why you are paid a director's fee; to be informed, to think and vote on all issues after a full and complete disclosure of facts. Facts may be obtained in written memoranda or the spoken word, and later recorded in the minutes of the corporation.

If the vote on an issue presented orally by the chairman takes place at the present meeting and you were not listening, access to minutes later becomes academic as far as the basis for your action on this issue at this time and in this meeting is concerned.

This chapter is a departure from our usual format:

1. State the challenge
2. Discuss how the challenge can be met
3. Report the results,

but its contents are deemed appropriate and useful in a text of this kind.

If you think about any of the comments or observations presented in this chapter prior to your next board meeting, the space in this book has been used to advantage.

Returning to the problem—solution—results format:

If a general problem exists regarding a director, it usually lies in one of these areas:

1. lack of preparation for the board meeting
2. inattentiveness at the meeting—not listening
3. lack of tact or misinterpreting combativeness for strength—lack of constructive cooperation.

In the area of Solution we have reviewed a formula or procedure followed by one of the most effective directors with whom it has been my privilege to serve.

As to Results, problems are not ignored, they are dealt with in a no-nonsense, sound and constructive manner.

While complete agreement has not always been present as to problem handling, there has never to my knowledge been any area of misunderstanding either. This is important and comes only as a result of deliberate and careful questioning with appropriate notes carefully made at the time of discussion.

Management needs a strong board and in considering candidates for future board membership, we have set out some primary factors that aid in the selection of these men over and above background and experience considerations.

PRIORITY SCHEDULE CONSIDERATIONS FOR IMPLEMENTATION OF NEW TECHNIQUES THAT RESULT IN MORE EFFECTIVE CORPORATE MANAGEMENT

Where to start; what sequence to follow; how to do it.

THE CHALLENGE

Now that we have reviewed and evaluated all of the new management techniques outlined in this book and we know:

- the management problems involved
- the solutions that work
- how to implement the proper new management techniques and
- the results that may be anticipated

we can sit back, relax and work out a logical sequence of implementation.

With a clear definition of company objectives in mind, we want to select, in sequential order, the use of those new management techniques that offer solutions to our most pressing problems. A reasonably accurate concept of the response time of your business to these new procedures or programs will be an essential part of your planning. Sequence will also vary in relation to company needs.

Ease and speed of implementation and the effect these changes have in improving return on investment are considerations.

If your company operates a number of divisions or branches, The Cost of Money Charge may be implemented quite readily with no investment and minimum risk.

This is a positive move to which your division management will be quite receptive.

If you are using a percent of sales formula now, it would be prudent to continue the same formula for several months, perhaps a quarter, with your accountant being instructed to prepare Cost of Money Charge figures on only your copy of monthly operating reports so that you can make some percentage and dollars and cents comparisons between the two charges. If comparative figures appear to be running at about the same level which should be in the area of 1% of sales each month, move to the Cost of Money Charge program after your next Division Manager's meeting, at which the new procedure would be presented with a well prepared "take home piece" outlining the procedure, how it works, and specifically what the manager can do to reduce the charge to his division. The theme of the memorandum should be built around the controllable nature of the charge and the fact that arbitrary allocations of corporate charges formerly made on a percent of sales formula will cease. Outline improvements expected. Be as specific as possible in each division. Monitor results and follow up with appropriate bulletins.

If inventory is a problem in any division, implement the Red Card System without delay. The procedure is simple.

Your company computer's capabilities and the availability of compatible in-store terminals would dictate the timing of initiating an Electronic Order Entry System. Check the feasibility with your Data Center Manager and consider costs involved in converting to the required equipment if conversion is necessary.

Make a Customer Evaluation Survey by volume categories in your company or in each of your divisions and have your operations people schedule order filling and deliveries accordingly.

The Design and Merchandising Department, Monthly Analysis of Operations and Planned Profit Programs for Customers, along with The Financial Services Manager, a New Concept in Credit Management are all integrated programs in which the Financial Services Manager plays a key role. Put your Credit Manager to work on these projects. If your present Credit Manager lacks interest or qualifications to do the job, look for a more alert, better qualified man. Begin a search for a qualified designer, draftsman, color coordinator and fixture man. One experienced man could qualify in all of these areas.

Make some preliminary contacts with reliable, even though small, fixture fabricating companies with a view of setting up a working arrangement for fixture fabrication and installation.

Open Performance Evaluation Files on your key employees with the view of using the files as a source of information for future management capability evaluations.

Regional management; do you have it? Is it functioning effectively? Do you have too many regions or too few? Do you need them at all?

Management by Objective can be used as an operating comparison tool with annual plans or objectives reported monthly in relation to accomplishment.

The Green Edge of Growth—it is more desirable to nourish growth and expansion from within your organization than to grow through merger or acquisition. In a business climate with interest in divestiture predominating, opportunities may exist to make your company better through an advantageous acquisition. This should be considered but you will seek to avoid any acquisition that results in making your company only bigger and not better.

An interested, helpful, thought stimulating Director is much more to be desired than an inattentive, combative one. The same principles apply in all company staff meetings.

It has been said that we learn slowly and that we put to use that which we have learned even more slowly.

I don't believe it.

Alert management is constantly in search of new, improved procedures, a better way with a cautious eye on sources and supporting facts.

Any constructive new management technique put to use anywhere in the business community enriches us all.

We learn from each other. Each one of us in management is indirectly the beneficiary of the creative thinking generated by other members of our peer group.

During the time spent with this book you have been in good company. You have been exposed to new and creative management techniques from a variety of exceptionally well qualified management and administrative people.

This is why this book was written and that is why you bought it.

You are far better qualified than anyone else to set up a schedule for implementing, in your business, the new management techniques outlined in this book. The schedule included in this chapter is by way of suggestion only.

Wherever you start and whatever sequence you follow, there is comfort and reassurance in the fact that a lowered working capital requirement for your company will result. Remember too, that you are not on new untried ground. It has all been done before and been done successfully.

In this book, you have all of the necessary tools:

- problem definitions
- solutions that work
- tools or forms to use
- results that may confidently be anticipated

To map out any new course of action and follow it through to a successful end requires some of the same courage and tenacity which any man in a pioneering effort needs. The business world has its victories but it takes strong men to win them. Individual leadership must be supported by an informed, intelligent staff dedicated from top to bottom to positive and successful applications of all new management techniques. With this support, you will gain the business victories you seek.

Progress—that is, true progress—is moving forward to improve the quality of what you are doing. Those who are honestly seeking real progress will find it in what is being done to improve competence at all levels of the business. Competence at the top is not enough nor is promotion to an upper job level necessarily a practical and just reward for competence at lower levels of responsibility.

Technological advances can enable you to reward people who are effective in what we have thought of in the past as lower level job responsibilities. Simply rewarding a person for competence in what he is doing may tend to keep competent people in all levels of your operation. Bright people seek to improve the degree of excellence in what they are doing.

All employees in a company do not necessarily equate progress in the company with promotion or moving up into unfamiliar job responsibilities that they can handle less well and with a lesser degree of personal satisfaction and pride of accomplishment. Is this contrary to historical business concepts that, in America at least, equate progress with promotion? Yes. Is it, therefore, in error or impractical? No.

Moving upward is not necessarily better. It can be worse. The proper viewpoint is for people to accept positions that are right for them and work toward a higher degree of excellence in those positions. Compensations, material and otherwise, should and will follow in the wake of these improvements.

The new generation now entering American business life understands this concept much better than its predecessors, and this realistic and constructive attitude just might start to improve things. The new breed of people are for the most part unimpressed by the culture in which people equate progress in a company and indeed, progress in life itself with moving upward. The changing of this viewpoint is basic and therefore important. In a sense, it is a phenomenon that provides a basis which people can accept and function effectively and happily in positions that are right for them. Many of the new management techniques outlined in this book will help do precisely that.

Malcontents may be upset with changing compensation levels that may result, but malcontents get upset with changes anyway and even with progress itself. Malcontents also can learn and most of them do.

17

NEW TECHNIQUES IN MERGERS AND ACQUISITIONS: THE GREEN EDGE OF GROWTH

The care and feeding of a "Growth Company."

THE CHALLENGE

In addition to favorable dividends or a good return on investment, people investing their money in a business enterprise want to see growth and expansion of the company in which their investments have been made.

How is this accomplished?

a. Growth and expansion from within through the use of after tax, after dividend retained earnings is obviously the most desirable growth pattern combined with the adequate financial planning and constructive corporate planning.

b. A merger or acquisition negotiated on a favorable basis is another desirable growth source provided the new acquisition makes your company better and not just a bigger one.

SOLUTION

Many of the new management techniques described in this book will aid in nourishing "the green edge of growth" described as the most desirable growth pattern outlined in sub-paragraph a. of this chapter.

New techniques in mergers and acquisitions constitute another approach to corporate growth.

If there was ever a period which saw a high degree of activity in the merger/acquisition area, and a raft of new techniques, it was the decade of the 1960's. Terms such as "conglomerate" and "project redeployment" came into being. Methods of financing the acquisition were varied and in many cases innovative, with various security packages utilized to accomplish the merger. One need only review the activities of companies such as IT&T, LTV, Teledyne, Litton and many others to see a wide variety of innovative ways to finance an acquisition.

If the 1960's belonged to the merger/acquisition experts, then the 1970's belonged to the operators. In this atmosphere, there has been less merger activity, but the opportunities still exist. Only the emphasis has changed. Whereas the first consideration of the 1960's was to see that the deal made sense financially, in the 1970's the overriding consideration was that it first must fit operationally. In fact, the merger activity of the 1960's supplies part of the current potential. Acquisitions made then may have never had operational compatability, or times have changed so they do not now. In any event, many diversified companies have divisions which are available.

At the same time, there continue to be independent companies which are seeking a merger partner. Their reasons are diverse, but quite often a primary consideration is simply growth or a desire by the controlling stockholders to diversify their investments, which usually can be accomplished by the receipt of either cash or a marketable security. The condition of the public stock market can have both a positive and negative effect on the financial aspects of acquisitions.

A generally depressed market probably makes it more difficult for your company to finance an acquisition; at the same time, the company you are seeking will find it even more difficult to utilize the alternative of a public offering, and the diversified company is not in a position to compete with an inflated equity.

The key is thus operations, more specifically an operational compatability, or, even better, a situation wherein your management can improve your acquisitions. The technique is to locate such a business and have the talent to analyze the operation and evaluate its potential *to you*. As for locating such a business, few "walk in the door." You need to seek them out and go after them. A major corporation often will not disclose, for various reasons, that a division is available. The owners of a private business, or the control persons for a smaller public business, may never think of merger until they are shown the benefits.

Oversimplified, there are three major considerations to a merger:

- the compatability of the operations
- the compatability of the people
- the ability to agree on a financial arrangement.

Too often, particularly during the 1960's, financing became the first, and in many cases, the overriding consideration. Admittedly, if financing cannot be worked out, the rest becomes academic. However, financing is only a means of payment, not the product itself. As in purchasing any item, the item must be beneficial to you before you consider the price. Only then do you determine the price you can afford to pay.

In summary, the 1970's did not see the furious merger activity of the prior decade, but opportunities still abound and on a more realistic basis. The technique is to identify those operations which can bring more benefit to you than your own internal growth.

There is an arsenal of new merger and acquisition techniques that came into existence during the 1960's. Some of these are presented for your review at the conclusion of this chapter if acquisition or merger is your interest.

Successful procedures used in my experience are outlined in the following paragraphs.

EXAMPLE "A"

The acquiring company which I represented was a large, multi-division drug distribution operation servicing a large region of the United States with a strong diversified economy and steady economic growth. The acquiring company's distribution pattern was incomplete in that one major market in the area was not covered. This area was serviced by a well established, highly regarded independent company operating three divisions, one of which was located in the same city and served the same market as a division of the acquiring company. Other competition existed in the principal city serviced by the major division of the acquired company.

Contact was made with the Federal Trade Commission through our attorneys and we were advised that we could not close the acquired company's division operating in the same city as one of the acquiring company's divisions and that this division would have to be sold to a competitor. This was no problem and after the acquisition, a satisfactory sale of the division was made to a competitor for cash.

The Federal Trade Commission required voluminous information which was accurately prepared and promptly supplied.

In negotiating the acquisition itself, in addition to the usual check lists and inquiries, there were four inventories or assets that were of primary concern.

These inventories were:

First, and most important, the people working for the acquired company. When it appeared that the acquisition would be consummated, I made arrangements, with the consent of the ownership/management of the acquired company, to visit and talk to every employee down to the level of supervisor. I wanted to test the "vibes." Some questions:

1. How do you feel about the merger of our companies soon to take place?
2. How long have you been with the company?
3. How long have you been on your present job?
4. What job did you hold prior to this one? How long?
5. What do you consider your next logical job promotion to be?

6. Do you have a job description of your present job? If not, will you write one for me?

7. Do you feel that changes will take place in the future that will be beneficial to you as an employee as well as good for the company?

At this point it should be emphasized that no representative of an acquiring company should ever make the statement that things will go on in the future as they have in the past and that no changes are anticipated. There seems to be an almost compelling tendency to do just this despite the fact that changes are certain to come from time to time and would occur even under the old ownership. After such reassurances, even the slightest change is magnified in importance and resented. We live in a world of change. Of course, changes are certain to take place if a business is to endure, but hopefully such necessary changes will benefit both company and employees alike. It is worth making a special point of this matter.

Second, if the "vibes" are right and I detect no resentment or overt opposition of significance, I proceed to the next most important inventory or asset—the merchandise inventory. I want to see not only the inventory listings and the figures in the accounting department, but I want to look at the merchandise itself, and I do. Handled tactfully, there is no problem here.

Third, accounts receivable aged analysis lists are helpful in evaluating accounts receivable worth as assets, but an examination of past payment trends by account, a review of correspondence files, and even a visit to stores where debt is high, if practical, is desirable. I made these visits ostensibly as "good will" visits, but also to look at the store, its inventory, its fixtures, the housekeeping and to make some kind of an appraisal of store ownership/management.

Fourth, buildings—have a look at the buildings themselves. Roofs, waterproofing, windows and plumbing vary as to condition. Age of a building alone is not necessarily a criterion of its condition, worth and possible future maintenance cost.

You say that asset appraisals are elementary, and this is true. But, you will avoid some unpleasant surprises by proceeding beyond just looking at paper. Mistakes that I have made as well as those of others with whom I have been associated, could have been avoided, by the simple process of "eyeballing" assets, physically and personally.

So much for this example.

RESULTS

The acquisition enriched the acquiring company with capable personnel and has become one of its largest and most profitable divisions.

This merger fit operationally and made the acquiring company better and not just bigger.

This acquisition has been reviewed in some detail because it is a good example of the results of carefully evaluating in the proper order of importance, these basic factors:

• compatability
• price
• quality of stock exchanged.

Compatability was the big essential here.

As for price, since the acquiring company's stock at the time of acquisition was selling at book value, an exchange of shares was made on the basis of book value of each company's stock. The acquired company was a privately held corporation with little or no market for its stock and no trading was taking place in it.

As for the third factor (quality of stock exchange), the acquiring company offered a marketable security (on a dollar for dollar basis). Since it was and is a publicly held company, this had appeal to the shareholders of the acquired company who could sell shares if they wished to diversify their investments.

Evaluating the acquisition in the light of subsequent experience, I consider the most valuable asset acquired to have been the "people inventory." Business is the doings of people and the experience and skills brought to the combined operation by this acquisition made immediate and substantial contributions to increased profits—well in excess of any dividend liability on the new stock.

The preceding example was of a very simple, uncomplicated acquisition. All circumstances and all factors involved indicated that a problem free acquisition or merger could be accomplished at that particular time. It was. All of these favorable factors are rarely present and a review of new techniques in mergers and acquisitions would constitute a valuable and useful addition to material previously given. Starting with the consideration of financing, we will review other aspects of this interesting subject.

As with all financing, the method used to finance an acquisition should be suited to the particular circumstances. There are a number of considerations which bear on any given transaction. For example, is the acquiring company publicly or privately owned? Is the company which is acquired public or private? What tax considerations are important? How important is marketability?

The combination of circumstances are innumerable, but some examples should provide ideas as to approaches which are possible. All examples used are ones wherein the acquiring company has public ownership and an active trading market, as this provides the greatest flexibility.

The most basic acquisition methods are (1) the purchase for cash and (2) the exchange of one equity for another. These are mentioned not only because they are widely used but also because most other methods are variations of one or both. For example, one simple variation of the cash method is to use as all or part of the consideration some form of debt of the acquirer. Other more complex variations are also possible, several of which were utilized and some even originated during the 1960's, often to meet a particular set of circumstances.

One vehicle used in certain instances is convertible preferred stock. Generally, such an issue pays a higher current dividend rate than the underlying common stock. It is convertible at some premium above the current market for the common, and has a senior balance sheet position to the common and some provision for required repayment. These features allow its use to meet one or more circumstance which may be present. For example, the current cash dividend on the acquiring company's common equity may provide a lower income level than the selling company's shareholder now receives, or would like to receive. A convertible preferred can be designed which provides the desired rate of income without the acquiring company's having to disturb its current dividend policy on the common.

Another use of the convertible preferred stock can be to reconcile a difference in opinion as to the relative value of the two companies (or more properly, the equities of the two companies), so long as the differential is not too great. For example, the common stock of the acquiring company is trading at $25 per share, and this company is willing to exchange one share for each share of the acquiree. However, the acquiree believes his stock is worth $30 per share. A compromise might be reached by exchanging $30 principal amount of a convertible preferred, convertible into one share of common. This is where the required repayment feature can become important. Even if the conversion feature never becomes of value, the seller will receive his $30 per share, with his only real risk being total failure of the acquiring company.

One possible shortcoming of the convertible preferred can be limited marketability, as there may be only a limited number of shares of a given issue outstanding. This was mitigated somewhat by certain companies actively engaged in acquisitions during the 1960's by using the same convertible preferred issue in two or more acquisitions.

Another variation used quite often during the 1960's was the contingent additional payment. This approach can be used whether the basic method is cash or stock, and it seems to have been used most often when the company to be acquired was showing relatively large increases in operating results. A common approach is to give a set amount initially, with an additional amount to be given over a period of, say, three years based on the amount that earnings exceeded a predetermined level.

Other variations have been included in recognition of the importance, in most instances, of the continuity of mangement. For example, in the acquisition of a public company, management personnel might receive stock options or other stock incentives in hopes of encouraging their continued activity and performance. In the acquisition of private companies even greater flexibility exists, including profit participations based on the results of the unit.

And, there are variations on variations. The acquiring company, rather than using a convertible preferred, may issue common, but give the holder some sort of a "put." This method carries with it contingent liabilities which one may fined unacceptable, but it illustrates the range of approaches actually used.

The eventual results of these many approaches to acquisitions are as varied as the methods used, ranging from situations wherein all parties are delighted through ones wherein one party is pleased but the other is not, to situations wherein all parties to the transaction wish they had never heard of one another.

Certainly, the eventual result in many instances was influenced more by operational than financial factors. However, an awareness of varied methods of handling the financial aspects of an acquisition can be helpful in actually enabling the completion of a merger, and such an awareness may also be beneficial to the design of a financial package which will prove suitable over the longer run to the owners of the company being acquired.

The "green edge of growth" will continue in the '80s for those companies with management employing *new, modern* techniques that result in increased sales and earnings while holding equity requirements at the lowest possible levels. A number of new techniques to accomplish this objective have been presented in this book. Growth from within through the use of after tax, after dividend liability, retained earnings is a sound way to go, but relatively slow and can be combined with selective acquisitions that meet desired criteria.

Unique special growth opportunities in the merger, acquisitions field will exist in the '80s. Prudent management will seek ways to generate more earnings from less investment within the bounds of reasonable risk factors. The '60s are past and the '70s (which are straightening out a lot of mistakes), are for the most part, in the record books too. So, learning from these experiences or the observation of the experiences of others, we can move into the '80s confident of what we want to do and knowing how we want to do it.

It has been the purpose of this book, written by experienced, professional management, to bring you knowledge that will prove to be useful in your business. We hope that you will accept our invitation to make use of those *new* management techniques that have aroused your curiosity. Your reward will be measurable improvement in management results. And it will happen much sooner than you expect.

If, in reading this book, you have gained the impression that reportorial work is minimal, confined primarily to essential statistical material and that we are thinking in terms of the future and not the past, you are with us all the way. Our concern is "what will work well tomorrow under conditions we are reasonably certain will prevail."

Where business was is interesting but academic. Many management techniques, methodology or tactics that produced acceptable results for generations past have simply no relevance to the future.

Doing more business profitably with less investment risk will be the dilemma and the opportunity for management tomorrow. Pressures from government, trade unions and the market place itself will continue and will grow in intensity. Some pressures will be more of what we already know and some will be new in origin. These pressures, of course, must be met effectively and constructively handled if a business is to endure and prosper.

A number of new tools have been placed on management's "work bench" in this book to aid in this task.

Again, we learn from each other. And in this process, we stand on the shoulders of many others.

18

RESULTS—THE LITMUS TEST OF SUCCESSFUL MANAGEMENT

A comprehensive evaluation of the bottom-line payoff from all new corporate management techniques described in this book working together over a 5-year period: Return on investment nearly doubled in 5 years as proven in the case of the "Fortune 500" company which achieved this record and is still growing. A figure-by-figure summary of all financial and operating specifics.

A 189% increase in R.O.I. in just five years was accomplished by Subject Company "E".

The Subject Company "E" study provides a complete field test and gives us an accurate overview of actual results obtained when all modern corporate management procedures outlined in this book are initiated and used consistently. This is not academic but actual application and consistent usage in the difficult arena of competitive American business. This is the real world of competition where stakes are high and there is little or no margin for basic errors in judgment. This is an actual company record. The period covered is five years. The fact that all new management procedures outlined work effectively and obtain highly desirable results is conclusive.

During the five year period of actual usage, all results were carefully monitored and verified. The arithmetic proved to be favorable.

Here are the results:

- SALES increased +85%
- EARNINGS (BEFORE TAXES) increased +180%
- R.O.I. increased +189%
- OPERATING EXPENSES decreased −30%
- NUMBER OF EMPLOYEES decreased −13%
- INVENTORY TURNS increased +22%
- INVENTORY OWNED BY COMPANY decreased −58%
- DAYS RECEIVABLES decreased −33%
- NUMBER OF ACCOUNTS decreased −40%
- AVERAGE ACCOUNT SIZE increased +209%
- TOTAL SQUARE FOOTAGE decreased −13%
- SALES PER SQUARE FOOT increased +114%.

Isn't that what you want?

- increased sales
- increased earnings
- more return on investment
- lower operating expenses
- fewer, more productive employees
- more inventory turns
- less inventory investment
- less investment in receivables
- larger, more profitable accounts to service and fewer marginal ones
- reduced warehouse and office space
- more sales per square foot of office and warehouse space
- in summary, more efficient and profitable use of equity?

Study the following chart and refer to those chapters having a direct bearing on each of these management controls. There you will find the source of each favorable management performance improvement.

The five year sales increase shown exceeds the industry average and is well ahead of market figures. Industry earnings figures are not even close to the favorable increase shown here.

The R.O.I. improvement is so dramatic that no industry, or trade area figures approach it.

Operating expenses at 7.2% of sales is a full 4 points better than the industry averages. Subject Company "E" operating expense percentages are continuing to improve. The trend is favorable while industry figures are moving in the opposite direction toward higher operating costs as a percent of sales.

Fewer employees, more inventory turns and reduced inventory investment is also contrary to industry trends during the period.

Fewer, higher volume, more profitable accounts constitute a trend that is working against industry patterns as is a reduction in operating space required to handle the business.

Sales per square foot are up more than 100% in five years. This is due partially to above average sales increases experienced each year for five years in servicing fewer but larger volume, more profitable accounts. It is also the result of a need for fewer employees to process the business in a smaller operating area.

Reference is made to the R.O.I. improvement. This does not mean that there was necessarily less capital employed in the business, but rather that less investment capital was required and used more efficiently and more profitably in relation to investment. A reduction in the percentage of inventory owned by the company helped as did a reduction in days receivables outstanding.

When the total square footage required to handle a growing business is reduced, so is your equity requirement to provide that space. Many things have worked together to attain a 189% improvement in R.O.I. in just five years. The preceding chapters tell you what these things are and how to apply them in your business.

Here is the schedule reflecting the five year operating results we have highlighted for you. Remember, these are actual operating results taken from audited statements. They are the "gut figures" that spell successful management.

Five Year Performance Record
Subject Company "E"

	First Year	Second Year	Third Year	Fourth Year	Fifth Year	5-Year Change
Net Shipments (000)	187,911	205,549	266,617	307,925	347,481	+ 85%
Earnings Before Tax (000)	2,777	3,455	6,078	6,734	7,788	+180%
R.O.I. (%)	9.0	12.1	22.1	24.0	26.0	+189%
Operating Expenses (%)	10.3	9.5	8.0	7.5	7.2	− 30%
Number of Employees	1184	1113	1094	1043	1033	− 13%
Inventory Turns	7.4	8.1	8.9	8.3	9.0	+ 22%
Inventory Owned by Subject Company "E" (%)	28.2	19.0	12.8	12.3	11.8	− 58%
Days Receivables (%)	36.7	32.1	26.7	26.5	24.6	− 33%

	First Year	Second Year	Third Year	Fourth Year	Fifth Year	5-Year Change
Number of Accounts (Active)	8,000	5,800	5,234	4,934	4,800	− 40%
Average Account Size/Yr ($)	22,078	33,373	47,935	58,688	68,144	+209%
Total Square Footage	912,355	886,455	864,141	864,141	790,141	− 13%
Sales Per Sq. Ft. ($)	193.60	218.36	290.34	335.09	413.97	+114%

This schedule is worthy of more than a cursory review. Study each result separately and carefully, then turn to the "how to" portion of each chapter that provides the basis for each accomplishment.

If your first reaction is "it can't be done," remember this is an actual case history, one of many. It not only can be done, it is being done successfully and profitably right now. As a person with management responsibility, you can do it too, but the answers are no longer in the old, familiar places. They may be found only in new concepts and innovative procedures that work.

A broad spectrum of exceptionally talented, creative management people with a high level of awareness and special insights into the causes of unprofitability and the reasons for profitability developed new management practices to correct the former and enhance the latter. These are the practices shared with you in this book.

INDEX

219